The Road to Derry County

the road to
DERRY COUNTY
an OZARK love story

Mark Allen Quay

Kamel press

Visit us at
www.MarkAllenQuay.com
to see more from this author!

Visit us at
www.KamelPress.com
to see more great books!

ISBN-13:   978-1-62487-103-0- Paperback
             978-1-62487-104-7- eBook

Library of Congress Control Number: 2023943742

Published in the USA.

For the hills, the streams, the forests, and,
above all, for my friends and family
who are always in my heart wherever I may be.

A Real and Very Short Prologue

This book arises out of three great loves: my faith, my family and friends, and the Ozarks. I could write pages and pages about the first two loves, but I think they come through well enough in this book about that third love—the Ozark Mountains of Missouri, my maternal homeland.

The reader may find this hard to believe but the stories in this book are true or would be true if someone had not done the math beforehand (you will see what I mean later). They have been told and re-told around campfires and woodstoves, maybe a little embellished over time, so make of that what you will. I guess you could say this work is sort of semi-autobiographical. As you would expect, the names, locations, and other identifying details have been changed to protect both the innocent and the guilty.

There are too many people I have to thank for their support, but I will mention a few here: my wife, whose patience and humor have always been sources of life-giving encouragement; my children, who heard these stories time and again while growing up and yet they still enjoy them; my many Ozark family and friends, especially the hillbilly mad scientists; Dr. Herb, who's always been ready to read and helpful to edit; and Tim, a true Southern gentleman, encourager, and friend. He's the one who did the math.

CONTENTS

Gettin' Your Bearin's Straight 1
   Alastair Spring 1
   The Ozarks: A Primer 4
   Derry County 6
The MacKays of Derry County 9
   The *Pater Familias* 9
   MacKay Family Reunions 16
   The Hungover Hound Dog 18
   The Ozark Farmer 23
"You Know, I've Been Thinking . . ." 24
   A Special Hole 24
   The Ford F-150 Trebuchet 29
   Homemade Artillery and Its Effect on Cows . . . 41
   Pig Fences May Fly 51
   Boiling Bobcats 73
   Chemistry and Chaos 77
Adele Crockett 83
Gimme that Ol' Time Religion 105
   The Rain Came Tumblin' Down 129
It's an Adventure .132
The Possum 151
Gimme that Real Ol' Time Religion 156
Nine: The Road out of Derry County 182
   Green Tea and Honey 182
   One Last Hike 188
About the Author 193

Gettin' Your Bearin's Straight

Alastair Spring

So, I guess this is by way of a prologue and you're probably tempted to skip it. I often pass them by myself in other books because they're usually full of the author's conceit and aren't much actual help. But, in order to understand the stories that follow, this brief chapter will, in fact, help, and you might even find it entertaining or at least interesting.

My name is Alastair Spring. On my dad's side, I'm descended from the Springs of Chestnut County, Pennsylvania, but, other than my dad, John, that part of the Spring family doesn't enter into these stories. My mom, Martha, was a Williams. Her dad was Charlie Williams, a postmaster, general store owner, and famed butcher. The Williamses are from Bean County, in the eastern Ozarks of Missouri, just to the north of Derry County (where most of these stories take place). People from all over Bean, Derry, and Rhett Counties used to come to Grandpa Charlie's store to get their cattle, hogs, and deer (the last only when in season, of course) butchered, neatly dressed out, and packaged in plain white paper, the name of the cuts and date of processing written in black ink in a pretty fair copperplate script. That is until the USDA stepped in and shut his operation down. He decided to retire from postmastering, store owning, and butchering, and moved to Oakmont, the seat of Rhett County, with my grandmother.

My mom's mother's name was Josie, not short for Josephine, as she was quick to tell. Her maiden name was MacKay, the surname of a large and prominent family that moved from Deer Lick, Tennessee, to Derry County in 1830. Her daddy was Cletus MacKay, a successful farmer and, even more importantly (as far as the menfolk in Derry County were concerned), a distiller of fine quality corn liquor. Her mom was Olivia Jones ("as was," folks today would say née), a fire-breathing, Bible-thumping, teetotaling Baptist. To this day, years after my great grandparents died, it was still a source of wonderment how those two ended up marrying. It was a successful marriage, for all that, as long as the subject of moonshine was avoided.

Cletus was the head of the clan, a role which his son, my great uncle, Mack MacKay, would assume after his daddy's death. Great grandpa Cletus owned most of the land along Derry Creek, a stream along which a community by the same name was situated. Cletus took good care of his own, but the country life was not what his daughter, my grandma Josie, had in mind, so she married at 16, moved into Providence (the county seat of Derry County), and happily helped Charlie run the butcher shop and general store (Williams' Meat and Sundries, sadly now closed).

My dad was an Army master sergeant who retired from the military in 1975. He married my mom, Martha, in 1958, while he was stationed at Fort Leonard Wood, Missouri. My mom was born and raised in Oakmont, which is just to the east of Derry County. They had three sons, of whom I'm the oldest. The five of us traveled around Europe and the US a good bit, giving me a much broader view of the world than my Ozark kin might have. When my dad retired, we settled in Oakmont where my mom's parents still lived. After high school, where I met and befriended some of the folks in these stories, I attended Missouri State University in

Springfield, graduating with a bachelor's degree in biology. After graduation, I joined the Navy and served for 23 years (retiring as a commander), during which time I got a master's degree in oceanography from the Naval Postgraduate School in Monterey, California. After leaving the Navy, I went back to school at the University of Missouri and got a Master of Education in teaching biology and, later, a PhD in science education. I taught high school biology, later went on to teach at community colleges and universities in Missouri, Arkansas, and even some short visiting professorships in Europe and Africa. I got hired as the Dean of the College of Education at Little Rock University, where I am today. Just prior to taking this position, I took a study sabbatical and went to Oxford, studying at Wycliffe Hall for a master's degree in Science and Religion, combining two of my great passions—the natural sciences and my Christian faith. I was raised Baptist, like most folks from the Ozarks, but later became a Lutheran (my father's childhood church) after a long theological and spiritual pilgrimage.

My wife, Elsbeth (an Oakmont girl), and I were married just before I went into the Navy. We have three children, two sons (Aaron and Ben) and a daughter (Naomi), and, as of this writing, seven grandchildren. Of course, being in the Navy, we traveled around a good bit and got to see a lot of the world. Both of my boys joined the military (one the Air Force, the other the Army), the seventh successive generation of men in my family to have served.

Over the years, Elsbeth and I would frequently go back to the Missouri Ozarks, visiting friends and family, attending reunions, and getting into some of the mischief (well, at least I got into such) that you'll read in these pages. Even with all my travels throughout the world, the Ozarks are still home. The mountains beckon to me with their silver green voices of spring-fed streams, tree-bedecked hills, and sheltered narrow valleys.

The Ozarks: A Primer

What are the Ozarks? The Ozarks, or the Ozark Mountains as they are often called, are a region consisting of two high plateaus (the Salem and the Springfield), two mountain ranges (the Boston and the St. Francois), and surrounded by rugged foothills, running from central Missouri in the north, to central Arkansas in the south, and from the eastern fringes of Oklahoma in the west to the Mississippi River valley in the east. The Boston Mountains portion of the Ozarks are the tallest mountains between the Appalachians and the Rockies.

Millions of years ago, much of the area was once covered by a vast, shallow inland sea. As its waters disappeared, it left behind a landscape dominated by limestone and dolomite, both highly dissolvable minerals. When rain falls on these minerals, a weak acid forms which erodes the stones, creating steep river valleys, rugged hillsides, and many caves. The eroded limestone and dolomite make the soils rich (especially in the river bottoms) but very rocky. Farming is the main occupation, and, if you can clear away enough rock, the sweet soil and plentiful water result in high yields. But that's difficult work, removing all those stones, so many farmers nowadays instead raise cattle that thrive on the abundant grasses which spring up readily from that fertile soil.

In the St. Francois (pronounced by Missourians as "St. Francis") range, you can find evidence of volcanic activity in the far distant past, leaving minerals behind like granite and rhyolite. Some locales here have large deposits of important metal ores, including iron, lead, and zinc, and even some silver. Their presence is important in Ozark history as many people, including Slavs from Poland and Russia, migrated there to work the mines.

Historically, this entire region was heavily forested by shortleaf and longleaf pines and various hardwoods, but the growth of the timber industry in the late 19th century resulted in extensive deforestation. Today, only about half of the pre-1870 wooded area is forested and very little of that by its original native pines unless it was replanted by the state or federal governments.

The Ozarks were extensively settled by several Native American tribes, the largest of which were the Siouan-speaking Osage. European settlement in the Ozarks did not begin in earnest until after the Louisiana Purchase in 1803. Prior to this time, French and Spanish prospectors, traders, and trappers ventured into the hills and valleys, but they left little behind except place names, like Fourche Creek, and legends of lost French or Spanish gold or silver. One such story, passed down in my family for at least four generations, tells of a lost mine and a stash of pure silver stored in oak barrels left by the Spanish in Derry County up close to the line with Bean County. It was a pastime for years for the menfolk in my family to go poking around in some of the narrow valleys (call "hollers" or "hollows") looking for purported mines. But mostly it was just an excuse to drink beer.

During the Jackson administration in the 1820s, the Cherokee were forcibly resettled in the region. This led to an ongoing war with the Osage in the middle of which the white settlers were often caught. The Cherokee did not remain for long, for they were resettled in the Indian Territory (Oklahoma), as were the Osage. Many an Ozarkan will claim "Cherokee blood," but if they have it, it was from the old Cherokee lands in the Appalachians from which many a settler came, since the Cherokee were not in this area for long.

Most Ozarkans are descendants of English, Welsh, and Scots-Irish families who migrated into this region during the 19th century from the Appalachians of Tennessee, Kentucky, Virginia, and North Carolina. The mountain-culture of the Ozarks nearly perfectly mirrors that of their old homes in the east. Many came to the Missouri Ozarks because the state of Missouri advertised extensively in newspapers nationwide to attract settlers, telling tales (mostly true) of the richness of the timber and the farmland of the area. To these folks, with their worked-over farms and depleted soil, the Ozarks sounded like a land of plenty. Well, it was a rich land, but its wealth was hard in coming.

Derry County

The MacKay branch of my mom's family came to the Ozarks from Derry County, Ireland, by way of the Carolinas and Tennessee, and were among the first white settlers in the area. They were a hard-bitten, hard-working clan of Scots-Irishmen. It was the head of the family, Iain MacKay, who named the county after his ancestral homeland. He established his family seat in the eastern part of Derry County along Derry Creek in 1830. In the western part of the county runs the largest river in the region, the Greystone River, along with one of its main tributaries, the Cave River.

It was on the Greystone that the town of Providence was built in 1835. It started with a small number of log buildings, including a courthouse, post office/general store, and a saloon. The latter, after ten years of temperance preaching by the Baptists, was closed. This, of course, gave rise to the extensive moonshine industry in the hills and hollers around the town.

Like the rest of the Ozarks, life in Derry County used to be difficult, brutal even. Farming, timbering, and raising children was tough work in its rocky valleys and ridges. Harvests would yield mostly stones and stumps at first. Only after years of toil would the rich, limestone soil along the creeks and rivers finally produce its bountiful crops of corn, sorghum, and the verdant pastures which fattened many a head of cattle.

In the late 19th and early 20th centuries, a company called The Providence and Oakmont Lumber Company, owned by a syndicate of New England magnates, brought good paying jobs, as well as healthcare and schools. Many men would leave off farming and go to work in the longleaf and short-leaf pine stands with two-man draw saws and double-bit-ted axes and float the newly cut logs down the crystal-clear Greystone River which wound its way through those rugged hills. When the forests were clear cut, and the hillsides left barren and eroded, these Yankee timber barons took their money on to the West, leaving behind boarded up schools and hospitals, and the Derry County man had to scratch out a living as best he could.

As I said, life in Derry County was hard. It's different today. City folks from St Louis, Kansas City, and beyond come to canoe and fish the Greystone and buy up all the handicrafts they can find at the Mercantile, much to Bat Simmons's (its owner) delight. These tourists come with their loud talk filling the Riverside Café, their loud music booming out of their cars as they drive through downtown Providence, and their loud money being splashed about for canoe and cabin rentals and on what they think to be excel-lent deals on quilts, homemade soap, bee's wax candles, and other folksy goods. The people of Derry County make a good living off these city folk. Many a St. Louisan or Kansas Citian think these folks to be ignorant hillbillies. Well, it is the city folks' dollars that line those hillbillies' pockets.

The stories I'm sharing with you are written in the manner of the Ozarks: tales which are often rambling, full of good humor, sometimes sad, and mostly just about life. Life, at least in the Ozarks, often doesn't have introductory para-graphs, thesis statements, or topic sentences. Life is often about nothing much at all and yet everything in general. Except when I'm quoting others, I've purposely avoided using the Ozark accent as much as I could to help the non-Ozark folks understand.

It's my hope that these stories will touch your heart, leaving you richer, happier, and more thoughtful, allowing the wisdom of these ancient hills to capture your imagination.

Alastair Spring, PhD
Dean, College of Education
Little Rock University
Grandchild of the Mountains

The MacKays of Derry County

The *Pater Familias*

My great uncle, Mack MacKay, was the *pater familias* of the MacKays of Derry County, Missouri. Just ask him and he'd tell you. It was a part of the small remnant of the Latin he learned in high school, but by God he knew that. He was the oldest, as well as the richest and most influential member of that extensive clan which settled in the eastern Ozarks of Missouri along Derry Creek. He was proud of his Scots-Irish heritage, though he was quick to say his name was not pronounced to rhyme with "eye" (as in Mack Eye), the Old-Country pronunciation, but rather it was pronounced to rhyme with "pay" as in Jim McKay of the old television show, ABC's *The Wide World of Sports*. Ignoring the extra "a," he frequently averred that he and Jim were cousins and he often quoted (too often for most folks) Jim McKay's famous saying, "The thrill of victory and the agony of defeat."

"Hey, Mack, understand yah got yer deer the first day o' the season."

"Yeah, but it was jist a little spike buck. As Ah was fixin' to drag him to the truck, out stepped the nicest eight-pointer yah ever did see."

"Oh, man, that's tough."

"Yep, as my cousin Jim used to say, 'It was the thrill of victory and the agony of defeat,'" not saying (but everyone in earshot knowing) he shot the other deer as well. He got the big buck tagged at the deer check station, but, little did the warden know, the other deer was under a tarp all the time. Hey, the little ones are the best eating.

Mack was six foot tall, right on the nail, but he insisted he was six foot one. Although not a particularly religious man, he believed the strange Ozark legend that the only man who was ever exactly six foot tall was Jesus. It was said it was the perfect height for the only perfect Man who ever lived. He didn't mind being taller than Jesus, so long as he wasn't the same height as the Savior. He was a rangy man, lean and, as they say, built of whipcord and baling wire. He was good looking too. His face was high-cheeked and darkly tanned. He claimed he was part Cherokee on his daddy's side, and, seeing him, you could believe it. His thick full head of hair was jet black, though in later life it would mellow to a salt and pepper. As he got older, he would walk with a tall man's stoop, but as a young man he stood ramrod straight, even before he went into the Army in 1942.

He was a talker, Mack was. He loved to tell stories, true ones if he had to, lies if he didn't. His tales were so good that it was the generally held conviction that if they weren't true, the world would be a better or, at least, a more interesting place if they were. While not often, his mouth would occasionally get him into trouble, especially with his wife, Sadie. But most of the time, an offer of "a swaller 'r two" from Mack's jug of the good stuff was enough to mollify even the most belligerent, again, especially Sadie.

Sadie was some 14 years younger than Mack. She was an Updike, one of the small groups of Dutch folks who moved into Derry County in the 1870s. She was a pale-complected woman with auburn hair. She was short in stature and had a short temper to go with it. It was said she had a tongue so sharp it could clip a hedge and make it shy of growing back.

Mack was usually a patient, slow moving man, never seemed in a hurry, but he would fly across the room and throttle any man who suggested anything at all was wrong with the MacKays of Derry County. But, for all that he was a slow-mover, Mack was nevertheless a hard worker. Unlike his good-for-nothing sons, there was not a lazy bone in his body. He kept sauntering along, from dawn till dusk, getting all his chores done with the greatest efficiency.

His farm was well-kept, nothing like his neighbors: no rusting trucks in the yard, house and barn always painted (white and red respectively, as they should be), no raggedy sofa on the front porch, no gates hanging off one hinge. His corn was planted in neat rows, his cattle were well-fed, and his chickens, by God, stayed in the pen, if they knew what was good for them.

He wished he could say the same about his sons, Ralph and Titus. He gave them each some land to farm, but the only things you could harvest out of their fields were rocks and thistles. What chickens they had were free-range back before it was popular. They weren't forerunners in poultry science, they were just bone idle (dumbass lazy was what most folks called them, if Mack wasn't within earshot). Mack spoiled his boys. He knew it, but don't you dare say it. He always gave them money, fixed their trucks, and made sure their families were well-clothed and fed. An otherwise frugal man, he was generous to a fault with family and friends.

Ralph and Titus were always together. They were big boys, didn't look a thing like their daddy. Tallish (though not as much as their dad), fat, and ill-favored. Even well into their middle age, they excelled at nothing except getting into trouble with the law. On Friday nights they were often liquored-up on their daddy's corn whiskey and they'd drive together into Providence and shoot up the traffic signs, streetlights, and the one traffic light in town. The sheriff would haul them into jail, and the next day Mack would bail them out. When it came time for their court appearance, in they would walk together in a straight line, Mack leading. He'd yell at the boys in front of the judge, promise he'd keep a tighter rein on them, and pay their fine. But for all his hollering and promising, Ralph and Titus would be back at their miscreant behavior within a week or so.

Shortly after I retired from the Navy, my wife, Elsbeth, and I drove up to Derry County to hike and canoe, our first time back in many years. One day we drove into Providence to eat at the Riverside Café. Best burgers in the Ozarks, they say, and they aren't far off. The café sat just off the courthouse square. As I was going into the restaurant, I looked around and saw the "O" had been shot out of a stop sign and there was glass littered around the base of some of the streetlights.

After lunch, Elsbeth and I walked across the street into the Mercantile, an old-fashioned general store, she to look at Ozark handicrafts, and I to talk to the owner, Bat Simmons, who was standing at his antique brass cash register. I remember him from my teenage years and early twenties, visiting family and canoeing, caving, and other outdoor adventures in the Ozarks. It being more than twenty years later, he probably wouldn't remember me.

Mr. Simmons's full name was Bartholomew Augustus Simmons, but who had time to say all that? He was called Bart by his folks, but long ago the kids on the playground at Providence Elementary School called him Batty Simmons and the name stuck, sort of.

Bat was a short, stocky man with slightly swarthy features. He would bustle around the store, keeping up an endless patter of small talk. For the tourists who frequented his store, he dressed up in old-timey garb, complete with pince-nez glasses, gray and black striped satin vest, black linen apron, and bright red satin shirt garters, always worn with a shirt of faultless white and crisply ironed gray or black trousers held in place over his paunch by buttoned red satin suspenders. He was bald-headed, except for a slight fringe around the sides and back. Regardless of the room temperature, his bald scalp always glistened with sweat.

"Mr. Simmons," I said, nodding politely. "I see the MacKay boys have been in town shooting the place up."

"Could be," he said suspiciously, narrowing his eyes. "Do I know you? Are you from around here?"

"I'm Alastair Spring, and I'm from Oakmont, more or less. My grandma is Josie Williams, Mack MacKay's sister, from over on Derry Creek. My wife and I were just over at the Riverside, and I noticed the stop sign and the lights."

Bat brightened up considerably. "Josie Williams. Ain't seen her 'n quite a spell. How's she doin'? And how's her ol' man, Charlie, weren't it? How long yah plannin' on stayin'? Yah still live in Oakmont?" As I said, Bat was a talker when he had a mind to.

"Well, grandma's fine. Nothing slows her down. Grandpa died last year. Heart attack. He was 83. My mom's her daughter, Martha. She married my dad, Ed Spring, from back east, who was in the Army, traveled all around the world." I mentally ticked off the answers to his questions. "My wife, Elsbeth, and I are just passing through. She's from Oakmont, too. Don't live there anymore. I was in the Navy, 23 years, and we traveled a bit too. Retired as a commander, went back to school, and started teaching science. I got a job at the university in Little Rock and settled there." I added the extra details because I knew he wouldn't be satisfied otherwise.

He nodded his head, taking it all in. "So, Charlie's dead. Good man. Yah know, he was the best butcher 'n three counties."

"Yes sir, and a good cook too, especially when it came to meat. He could bake a ham and then slice it by hand so thin you could hold it up to the window and see the sunlight coming through."

Bat laughed. "Well, anyhow, y're right about Ralph and Titus. They came in Friday night, drunk as skunks, and began shootin' things up. Said they was sightin' in their new deer rifles, Remington 30-06s. Said they couldn't help it if there was no other targets. Sheriff Connelly threw 'em in jail and called their daddy. Mack said he wasn't goin' to bail 'em out this time."

"Did he?"

"No, he didn't. He waited till Monday an' went into the court with the boys. Yelled at Ralph and Titus, yelled at Judge Williams for raisin' the fine from last time (I couldn't rightly blame the judge), and yelled at Connelly for confiscatin' their rifles. 'How they supposed to feed their families iff'n you go takin' away their rifles?' As they was a leavin' the court, Mack cuffed them each upside the head. Here they are, goin' on 40 years old, and he's a whoppin' them like they was 10 year old boys. I dare say they deserved it, but Mack does spoil them good fer nuthin' idjuts."

Mack MacKay's actual given names were Walter Ovid, as in Walter Scot (the author of *Ivanhoe*) and the Latin poet, Ovid. His daddy, Cletus, was something of a reader (what time he wasn't minding the farm or making 'shine). But those names just wouldn't do. Not in the eastern Ozarks, not in Derry County, not along Derry Creek, and by-damn certainly not amongst the august company of corn engineers whose dedication to their craft resulted in so many shotgun weddings. But "Mack" worked just fine.

Prior to going off to France in World War 1, Cletus got as far along in his education as you could back then in Derry County, which is to say eighth grade. He valued education and loved to read. He insisted that Mack go to high school and rode him hard to make sure he graduated. He did, with honors. Mack shared his daddy's love of learning and reading, and it was one of his great sorrows that Ralph and Titus were practically illiterate. He tried to make them stick it through high school, but they dropped out, more interested in fishing and hunting and girls (not that any girl would ever give them a second look). As I said, he spoiled those boys.

As you've probably figured out, another way in which Mack took after his daddy was the illegal manufacture and sale of corn whiskey. During the Prohibition, Cletus made a good deal of money running a moonshine still back up at the far end of Derry Creek. It was good stuff, too. Most 'shiners make two batches of whiskey: the "good stuff" for kinfolk and friends (meaning it was aged for at least three months and they used *bona fide* copper tubing for the condenser) and "rot gut" for everyone else. There was always a suspicion that a car radiator (which has lead) was used as the condenser for the rot gut. Not so with Cletus and Mack. All their moonshine was the "good stuff."

Word of the quality of Cletus' product got around. One day some men from St. Louis drove up to his farmhouse in a fancy brand new Packard Victoria. They wore expensive gray pinstriped, double-breasted suits, shiny leather shoes with gray silk spats, starched white shirts with red silk ties, and broad-brimmed black fedoras. They offered to buy every drop he could make. Offered good money too. Being an intelligent, shrewd man, Cletus drove a hard bargain and got them to come up another dollar and a quarter per gallon jug. It was the mark of how good the stuff was that they agreed, after some reluctance and a bit of "see here" and "where do you get off" and "now let's be reasonable."

Cletus was able to get away with his distillery operation because, with a nod and a wink (and a pint or two a week), Cletus got the sheriff to look the other way. He gave him a whole gallon jug when the sheriff warned him about the Revenue men.

Mack took over his daddy's trade. Even after Prohibition, he still made good money. For a while. But tastes change and Jack Daniels is easier on the palate (if not on the wallet). He continued to run the still, as much for old time's sake as anything. His daddy would probably roll over in his grave, up on Piney Bluff where the MacKay Cemetery sat, if he were to stop.

MacKay Family Reunions

The MacKay Cemetery was the site of the annual MacKay family reunion, usually on Memorial Day. The MacKays would come from all over Missouri, Arkansas, and beyond. First, the family would clean up the graves, removing last autumn's leaves, weeds, and poison ivy, and thinning out the irises and peonies. They'd put flags on the graves of veterans, and Mack always made a show of saluting his daddy's grave. Then they'd walk around reading the tombstones, sharing stories, laughing, and crying. Later, after lunch, some of the folks would get out their guitars, along with a mandolin or a banjo or two, maybe even a fiddle, and there would be music with bluegrass and old-time country gospel standards.

After the graves were cleared, they would have lunch, setting up boards on sawhorses for tables (everybody would bring their own lawn chairs), covering them with red and white checked tablecloths, and laying out a feast as only Ozark women can make. There would be deviled eggs (my favorite), fried chicken (of course), home-canned green beans with new potatoes, potato salad (lots of mayo), macaroni salad (even more mayo), broccoli-cauliflower salad (with mayo and lots of bacon), Jell-O salad, and wilted lettuce (a divine combination of chopped red onions, sliced radishes, and bibb lettuce over which hot bacon fat was poured—try it before you turn your nose up at it). Even into the 1990s, no one in the MacKay clan ever heard of low-fat, or if they had heard of it, they were pretty sure it was a government conspiracy. For some, the highlight of the picnic was Aunt Sadie's chocolate soak cake.

Now, before I talk about that cake, I need to talk about the great family divide. The MacKays were not by disposition especially church-going folk. Oh, they'd go for Christmas and Easter, maybe the Vacation Bible School pageant. They'd show up for a wedding or a funeral. Might even saunter down to Derry Creek to watch a baptizing. Maybe even go to a brush arbor meeting and get religion for a little bit. But as a rule, they figured that they and God were on pretty good terms, and there was no need to formalize that relationship.

However, Grandpa Cletus's wife, Olivia Jones (as was), was a teetotaling, Bible-thumping, hell-fire-and-brimstone, a-hollering and a-shouting, clapping to the old time Stamps Baxter hymns, fundamentalist Baptist. All the Joneses were. It regularly broke great grandma Olivia's heart that Cletus wouldn't give up his evil ways and even more so when her baby boy, Mack, took up the devil's occupation of making corn whiskey.

The Jones family hung around the MacKays, shaking their heads at their goings-on, but showing up at the reunions, nevertheless, eating their food, and burying their dead in the cemetery. The "fact" of moonshine was there, an unspoken dividing line, so much so that the MacKays sat at one end of the tables and the Joneses at the other. It wasn't the MacKays insisted on this partition, but they did nothing about it since it seemed to make the Joneses more comfortable.

Now, back to that cake. The cake itself was just an ordinary, Duncan Hines devil's food cake. The secret to its greatness was the two cups of corn liquor poured over the cake after it had set cooling a spell. The cake would soak up all that moonshiney goodness and blend it all together to create a taste nothing short of heaven (heaven, that is, if the Joneses were wrong and God was not a teetotaler).

As soon as the cake was uncovered, the Joneses would forget all about their concerns about the MacKays and come tumbling over each other to get a piece of that cake. I made the mistake once of trying to explain to my Aunt Dorothy, one of the Jones clan, that there was whiskey in the cake and wasn't that against her religion?

"No, now, thet alcohol gets all baked out of that cake. What's left is jist a little flavorin', like cookin' sherry."

I decided not to press the matter any further. Seeing how happy everyone was after eating a piece of that cake, I figured sometimes ignorance truly is bliss.

The Hungover Hound Dog

There's nothing more mournful than a hound dog with a hangover.

Well, I guess I better explain myself. I was at a family reunion at the MacKay cemetery. We had finished clearing the graves and cutting back the botanical invasion from the adjacent forest and were sitting down for the picnic lunch. Across the table from me was my aunt Zonie. Her name was actually Arizona (no kidding), and her sisters were Tennie (Tennessee) and Minnie (Minnesota). She wasn't actually my aunt, more like a second cousin a few times removed, but she was quite a bit older than us Baby Boomers, and "cousin" Zonie didn't seem quite right, so Aunt Zonie it was.

Aunt Zonie was always full of family stories which she loved to tell, and as a writer, I loved to listen to her and even take a note or two for the family history I was working on sporadically over the past five years or so. This year was no exception.

Those of us clustered around Zonie at one end of the table were talking about dogs, breeds, and hunting dogs, and so forth. I wasn't a dog owner at the time, so I didn't have much to contribute. It was in the middle of this conversation that Zonie made her solemn pronouncement, "There's nothin' more mournful than a hound dawg with a hangover." Well, that couldn't go unexplained, so we began clamoring for the story behind her statement.

The way Zonie told it, it seems her daddy, Virgil MacKay, bought two coon hounds. Treeing walkers they were, and mighty expensive. Virgil went to a champion breeder down in Pocahontas, Arkansas, and paid $50 apiece for them, a princely sum for the 1930s. True to the breed type, they were both tri-colored: a brown, tan, and white one named Zeke, and a blue (actually, a gray, but they call it blue), tan, and white one named Old Blue.

Now, Old Blue was a coon hunting fool. He wasn't happy unless he was out hunting with Zonie's daddy, and when Virgil came in from the fields, after he washed up and had his supper, he'd take his old red coal-oil lamp and his thumb-cocked shotgun, and give a call, "Boo-ha! Here Blue, here Blue! Boo-ha!" Out from under the front porch, where he'd been lying out of the sun, would come Old Blue, baying and yapping like he just earned a million dollars on the Chicago commodities exchange, "Boh-woh-woh-woh! Boh-woh!" Off they went into the woods and often they weren't back till well after midnight. In the distance you'd hear Old Blue clear as a bell, "Boh-woh-woh! Woh-woh-woh!" and Virgil would call after him, "Hoo Blue! Hoo Blue! Get 'em Old Blue!" When the hound treed a coon, you'd hear him change his tune. "Boh-woh! Boh-woh! Arp, arp, arp! Huff-huff-huff! Boh-woh!" Virgil answered, "Get 'em up, Blue! Woo-hoo, get 'em on up there, Blue!" Let me tell you, on a moonlit night in October it was sure enough the most beautiful music a body could wish for.

Well, what about Zeke? Hah! He was surely the most disappointing treeing walker in the history of the breed. Zeke was what they used to call an "egg-suckin' dawg," which is to say a dog so lazy he'd rather wander into the hen house and raid the nests than work for his room and board. Zeke didn't actually suck eggs, but dispositionally, he was a sure enough, *bona fide* egg-sucking dawg.

One day, Zonie's cousin, Marybeth Jones, was visiting. Folks often used to visit with relatives a week or two, help out around the farm, and generally entertain the host family with tales as to what others, related or by way of being family friends, got up to.

One morning during her visit, Marybeth and Zonie were cleaning up after breakfast, her daddy having headed off to the barn to try and start the old blue Ford tractor for the day's chores. They had half a cast-iron skillet of cat's head biscuits left, which Zonie started to take out to wrap in a moist dishtowel to serve later at dinner (what city folk call lunch).

There needs to be a word of explanation here about cat's head biscuits. Some people call them spoon biscuits or spoon bread. The idea was instead of making a stiff dough, rolling it out, and cutting it with the lid of a Mason jar (or such like), you'd make a batter, thicker than pancake batter, and spoon it into a skillet (greased with lard or bacon fat, thank you very kindly), each dollop being about the size of a cat's head, thus "cat's head biscuits."

So, back to the story. Zonie heard a "Wuff!" at the screen door off the kitchen. There was Zeke, eyeing Zonie and eyeing the biscuits, and making pleading little wuffs and whines, indicating those wonderful breakfast concoctions would sit better in his stomach than elsewhere.

"That good fer nothin', egg-suckin' dawg," said Zonie derisively.

I was not aware of Zonie's mischievous, not to say mean, streak. Well, it sure came out in this story. Zonie turned to Marybeth and said, "Hey, watch this."

She went over to the fireplace, reached behind the mantle clock, and brought out a small bottle of her daddy's cousin Cletus's "good stuff." This was for medicinal purposes only, of course, and which was refilled from a gallon jug Virgil kept in the spring house. She poured some of that fine Ozark corn liquor into the frying pan with its remaining cat's head biscuits and let it absorb completely. She went over to the screen door, propped it open, and threw a whis-key-soaked biscuit to the dog.

Zeke eagerly snatched the biscuit out of the air with a resounding "Wop," swallowed it quickly, blinked, and leaned slightly to one side as the heat of the moonshine worked its way from the back of his throat to his stomach. He must have liked it, for Zonie kept chunking biscuits at him, and he would snag them while in flight, each time leaning a little more toward the horizontal and alternating sides so that he was like a fur-covered pendulum.

About the time Zonie had thrown the last biscuit, a chicken, who somehow managed to give its pen a slip, happened by and said something rude to the dog. Zonie and Marybeth didn't quite catch it, but it must have been very rude indeed, for Zeke took considerable exception to it and started chasing the chicken. Of course, it could be that the chicken didn't say much more than "Howdy, Zeke," and the dog, in a drunken state and hearing an insult where none was actually intended, replied, "What'cha mean by thet?" and gave chase. Whatever was the case, it was obvious to Zonie, Marybeth, and the chicken, that Zeke was a mean drunk.

The dog started chasing the chicken 'round and 'round the house, both neither gaining nor losing any ground to the other. The girls were truly taken aback by the course of events and began to wonder about the wisdom of feeding moonshine-laden biscuits to dogs, egg-sucking or otherwise.

Now, dogs slobber considerably when they are exercised over some matter, and, apparently corn liquor, even "the good stuff," doesn't agree with the mouth and throat of a dog, so that Zeke slobbered even more than usual. This, combined with the hard breathing brought about by an out-of-condition hound pursuing the impertinent fowl, created a rich, creamy froth around the dog's mouth.

It was at this time that Zonie's daddy came up from the barn, having fixed the tractor, to get a drink of water before heading back to hitch up a plow. Virgil came to a sudden stop and watched with no little surprise and concern as Zeke chased the chicken, displaying an industry never before witnessed. After a moment, his keen hunter's eyes spied the foam around the dog's mouth and the girls standing with shocked expressions in the kitchen doorway, added the matter up, and diagnosed the situation.

"Girls!" he shouted. "Get in the house and shut all the doors. Ol' Zeke's got the ray-bees."

It was with considerable emotion, no little wheedling, and a great amount of omission of the truth, that Zonie and Marybeth convinced Virgil to lock up Zeke in the old henhouse. The idea was if you shut up an animal for a couple of weeks, and he didn't die, he probably didn't have rabies. Virgil had to wait until the chicken finally managed to escape the race and Zeke to fall in a disgusted heap on the porch before he could get a loop of rope around the dog's neck and drag his reluctant carcass to his makeshift jail.

It later occurred to Virgil that there might be a liquid cause to Zeke's condition, a liquid administered by a certain two young ladies, but Zonie had surreptitiously refilled the bottle on the mantlepiece from the jug. Finding the bottle full, Virgil reckoned, "It's jist one of those things. You jist never know with dawgs." Perhaps especially with egg-sucking dawgs.

That evening, there was the mournfullest cry coming from the old henhouse. "Boh-woo! Woo! Woo! WOO! Boh-woo!"

Like she said, there's nothing more mournful than a hound dog with a hangover.

The Ozark Farmer

Across the miles that are years,
over Indian-named rivers of tears,
down the rutted roads of experience
to where the trumpet creeper's orange blaze
peers through its clay-dusted haze—
speak now of loves that abound
far, far beyond mere seeing or bare sound:
earth, corn, cattle, split wood, and sweaty brow,
aching back, dirt beneath the fingernails,
knotted muscles; he prevails
    and touches in the seasons
    eternity's slow harvest.

By this is Eden reborn:
in tilling, planting, and reaping the corn
measuring the cycles of times and troth
and love in his keeping, pacing the toil
with stone-scuffed boots, ground-in soil,
mismatched patches on his knees.
As he follows the mules with haws and gees,
plowing the dirt of his hard present time,
what hill-born philosophies does he dream
in the Ozark noon-light beam,
    turning the furrows in a
    joyful hope of tomorrow?

"You Know, I've Been Thinking . . ."

A Special Hole

It's been said by many a Missourian or Arkansan that the most dangerous words in the Ozarks are, "Here, hold mah beer." As in, "Here, hold mah beer and watch while Ah do a wheelie with mah ATV." Or "Here, hold mah beer. Ah gotta shift 'er down real low 'cause o' this grade. Brakes ain't so good on ol' Bessie." Or "Here, hold mah beer while Ah shoot that skunk." Okay, the last one is probably more stupid than dangerous. Except for the skunk.

But I can tell you for a fact the most dangerous words in the Ozarks are when an educated hillbilly—a mountain mad scientist, as it were—says, "You know, I've been thinking..." Here's an example.

There was a group of us huddled together around a hole. That's right, a hole. This was a special hole. What made it special? Well, three reasons.

First, it was at the base of a cliff, maybe 90 or so feet high, which had once been the back wall of an enormous cave. Over time weather, geology, chemistry, and gravity had done their work. Now all that was left was a cliff. Oh, and the hole. What mysteries could that hole lead to?

Second, the hole was special because further up on the cliff, say around 75 feet, there was a small cave that went back maybe 50 feet. Not a very long cave, granted, but a cave, nevertheless. Were the hole and the cave once connected? I'll save the story of getting to that cave for another time.

There was one more reason why the hole was so special. It was a cold winter day, just above freezing, when we gathered, shoulders hunched in our time-worn, adventure-stained jackets, hands in our pockets. The air was crisp and dry. And out of that hole was pouring a steady stream of warmish, moist air. It looked as though a cloud was rising out of the hole. Those in the group who were experienced cavers (which included me, by the way) knew that meant only one thing: there was a big, deep space on the other side to warm the air and saturate it with water vapor. Did I say the hole was special?

We wondered what that hole might lead to. A cavern filled with curtains of amber calcite? Deep, underground lakes populated with eyeless, ghostly pale Southern cavefish? Crevice-lined hallways populated with blind, pinkish-colored grotto salamanders? The legendary lost Spanish mine? The buried silver of some panicked French explorers fleeing from the Osage? Yes, it was a special hole indeed.

The opening of the hole was a nearly perfect circle. It was set at a bit of an angle at the cliff's base, surrounded by break-down from the cliff face. It was only about two and a half feet across and was lined with sharp rocks and red clay. It was barely big enough to belly crawl in. We did. Or we tried to. About six feet in, there was a column formed by the joining of a stalactite with a stalagmite. It bisected the hole neatly in the middle and there was no going around it. We all tried in turn. Well, some of us made the effort. A few of us (won't mention any names) were a little too big in the waistline. Each time, we were confronted with that stubborn pillar, and it was not budging. It did not care that it was obstructing our investigation of that special hole. In fact, it didn't care about much of anything.

Let me go back and talk about "the group." We were all "mountain mad scientists." Some of us lived in the Ozarks year-round. Others came from the area and would come back to visit family now and again. I lived in Little Rock at the time, but my family has lived in the eastern Missouri Ozarks since the 1830s. What distinguished this group from most other hill folks was that we were educated. Very educated. All of us had at least one graduate degree with three PhDs thrown into the mix. There was a state biologist, a retired psychologist, a junior high principal who once taught science to grades 6-8, a high school math teacher, a professor emeritus of physics, a journalist, and a former Navy marine scientist who was the dean of a college of education (yours truly), enough to provide half the faculty for a small community college. Some of the finest minds in all the Ozarks were gathered around that hole. Did I mention it was a special hole?

It was at this point the "You know, I've been thinking . . ." started. It was Steve, the clinical psychologist, who was retired from the state mental hospital in Farmington, Missouri, who led the way. "You know, I've been thinking that maybe, with a two-pound sledge and a chisel, we could bust that column right outta there." We all agreed that was a good idea. We also agreed that Steve should be the one to try. After all, he'd been the one thinking.

Ed, the physicist, who used to be a professor at Missouri State University, said he just happened to have those two things in his pickup. He hitched up his jeans and sauntered over to the truck. The truck was a blue-gray Chevy Silverado, and its paint had seen better days, like maybe fifteen or twenty years ago, which was odd since the pickup was only about ten years old. Ed dragged a banged-up, rusty toolbox from behind the frayed driver's seat, rummaged around a bit, found the sledge and chisel, sauntered back (we do a lot of sauntering in the Ozarks), and handed them to Steve.

Steve looked at them. We could tell he was thinking. Probably, "There's a lot of rust on these. I wonder if my tetanus booster is up to date." Finally, shrugging his shoulders, he took off his St. Louis Cardinals ball cap and crawled into the hole. Did I mention it was a special hole?

We heard a slight tap as he set the chisel. Then another tap. Then a blistering string of profanity poured out of that special hole. Out came Steve, covered in red clay, holding up a hand that was purplish red and already swollen.

"You know, I'm thinking that hand's gonna be black and blue before the day's out," I observed.

Steve glared at me and then at the others when they began to laugh. He let out another long stream of expletives. (It was satisfying to note that the old Freudian expressions were still in use by shrinks.) It seems there wasn't enough room down there to get a proper swing, so the sledge and chisel slipped, and Steve's hand, which had not been thinking of anything much at all, took the brunt of that slip.

"Okay," snarled Steve, "if you guys are so smart, what do you think we should do?"

Then came the next "You know, I've been thinking . . ." It came from Ed, on whose farm the cliff and the hole were located. "We can take a long prybar, the kind with a chisel point, put it down into the hole, and hit it with a bigger sledge from the outside. Pretty sure I've got those back at the farm." What a great idea!

So, Ed sauntered from the hole (did I mention it was a special hole?), hopped into his pickup truck, and pulled out, spraying red clay mud, while several of us tried to clamber into the back. Most of us made it. The few who didn't decided they'd rather stay huddled around the hole anyhow. It was a special hole, after all. We arrived at his ramshackle farm and began scouring his gloomy tool shed and even gloomier barn for the necessary implements. We found all sorts of things: deer antlers, cobwebs, deer hides (not cured, ugh!), rusty pliers, cobwebs, rusty saws, a rusty hammer with a broken handle, cobwebs, a lot of screw drivers (also rusty), piles of moldering physics textbooks, and cobwebs. But no sledge of any kind (bigger or not) and no chisel-pointed prybar.

"Coulda sworn I had those things," said Ed, apologetically. One more "You know, I've been thinking . . ." bit the dust.

We drove back to the hole, that special hole, bumping along in the truck bed, quietly considering what we'd think of next. When we arrived, barely had we jumped out of the pickup when we all began throwing out ideas.

"We could bring in a backhoe and dig it out," offered a local high school math teacher named Ian, scratching his balding scalp meditatively.

"No, that might disturb critters in there," said Mike, the biologist, who worked for the Missouri Conservation Department. "Maybe bats." (Critters being the Ozark scientific term for cave fauna.) "Besides," he continued, "we couldn't drive one close enough to the hole."

"We could look for another opening," offered Carl, the journalist. He worked for the News Tribune in Jeff City.[1] Leave it to a non-scientist to come up with a sensible idea. Come to think of it, Carl never says, "You know, I've been

---

[1] Jefferson City, the state capital.

thinking . . ." But three hours of hard scrabbling yielded no undiscovered entrance.

So, we stood around the hole again, the warm, moist air billowing around us. Did I mention it was a special hole? Finally, Allen, the principal at the local junior high, said, "You know, I've been thinking . . ." He was looking off into the distance while scratching his chin thoughtfully. We held our collective breath: here it comes. "We could use a half stick of dynamite to blow that hole open."

We all looked in stunned amazement at Allen. This was the man who suspended boys all the time for throwing firecrackers into the staff room and flushing M-80s down the toilets. Now he was suggesting dynamite?

Shaking his head in disbelief, Ed said, "Allen, that's the dumbest idea I've ever heard of. First of all, we don't have any dynamite, and secondly . . ." But that was as far as he got. We all busted up laughing at the ridiculousness of the idea, and soon, even Allen joined in. One by one, we gave the hole a last glance, shrugged, and climbed into Ed's truck, probably sauntering in the process.

Dynamite? Hey, the hole was special, but not that special.

The Ford F-150 Trebuchet

I mentioned earlier about the small cave on the cliff face up above the special hole and I promised I'd tell you the story of how we tried to get to it. So, here it is.

If the story told about this small cave is true, it was special, kinda like the special hole, in its own right. The story goes that a hunter by the name of Ralph MacKay (a cousin of mine, you may recall) had a black and tan coon hound who wandered off into Stringfeller Creek Hollow, which leads back to Stringfeller Cavern. Ralph thought he heard an oddly tinny bark from the dog and reasoned that it might have journeyed into the cave. Damn dog.

Stringfeller was no small cave. From a tight hole, barely big enough for a good-sized man to squeeze into, it opened up quickly into a largish cavern some 15 to 20 feet high (with some rooms measuring over 50 feet). There were multiple side passages, underground streams with waterfalls, incredibly beautiful crystal-clear water hemmed-in by rim dams, and black-flecked amber calcite stalagmites, stalactites, and columns. Oh, and red clay mud on the floors. A lot of red clay mud. The main passage went back for at least a mile and a half, and the side passages probably added another mile or two to its overall length. No Carlsbad Caverns, certainly, but also no short, gravelly grotto either.

Ralph knew he couldn't venture very far into the cave because the main passage veered sharply to the left after about 20 feet. Sunlight from the mouth of the cave didn't go very far and he didn't have a flashlight on him. Ralph stood at the entrance, bellowing and whistling, alternatively cajoling, commanding, and cursing the dog. Nary a sign. He thought he might have heard a small bark, far off down the passage.

Ralph turned to head back to his truck to see if maybe he had a flashlight. He started up the path going from the cave mouth back to the hollow. He slipped on the red clay mud that covered the path, twisted his ankle, wrenched his knee, and, as he fell, he banged his shoulder against a rock. A big rock. A big damn rock. And damn the dog, too.

Ralph could barely pick his way out of Stringfeller Creek Hollow and return to his beat-up green Ford F-150 pickup, which was parked at the opening to the hollow. There was no way he was going to get a flashlight, if he had one, out of the glove compartment and go back for that coon dog. That worthless hound could find his own way home.

The dog did show up three days later, covered in red clay mud. Ralph sulked for days about his ankle, knee, and shoulder. Well, anyhow, it got him out of work, something which pleased Ralph highly.

Thus far, the story rings pretty true. A lotta folks knew Ralph and even knew the dog, and everything seemed completely plausible.

Then Ralph started "storyin'" a yarn which no one believed. Ralph certainly gave every sign he believed it to be true, but it's widely known amongst Ozark storytellers that a lie, repeated often enough, soon takes on a veneer of truth so convincing that eventually even the liar comes to believe his tale is absolute gospel.

So, what was his story? It was that, earlier on the same day that the black and tan hound came home, he was seen (by whom he didn't say) standing in the opening of the small cave in the cliff face. Amazing! Incredible! Couldn't be true, but . . .

Ralph reasoned that the coon hound worked its way to the very back of Stringfeller Cavern by scent and sound alone and found a connecting passage that led all the way to the cave. When the hound arrived at the opening, he found a sheer cliff face, reasoned with his doggy reason there was no viable way down from there, and turned around and retraced his tracks. Smart dog. But still, a damn dog.

Well, Ralph was convinced, or at least allowed as he was convinced, and began spreading the tale at the Riverside Café, in the Mercantile, in the courtroom while explaining to Judge Williams why he hadn't paid his fine for shooting out the glass of the heavily curtained windows of the Masonic hall ("What'er they hidin' anyhow, yer honor?"), and in Hiram's Barber Shop (been in business for 50 years in the same location with the same name, so the current owner is not named Hiram; who names their kids Hiram, nowadays?).

Ed overheard Ralph at the Riverside Café while he was finishing his last cup of coffee over that day's edition of the St. Louis Post Dispatch. Allen listened in as Ralph shouted his story over the hoots and hollers of patrons at Hiram's. Bat Simmons took stock of Ralph's obviously lying yarn (obvious to Bat, anyhow) before he threw Ralph out of the Mercantile. And Ian happened to be standing outside the courtroom when the "conversation" between Ralph and the judge took place. Ian never let on as to why he was in the courthouse himself.

On a Fourth of July weekend, over beers and barbequed burgers at Ed's place, we mountain mad scientists discussed Ralph's story about the caves and the damn dog.

Ed said, "Before I left the Riverside, Ralph came up to me and asked, 'Ed, you believe me, don'tcha? You know caves. Yer a scientist. Hey, the little cave on the cliff is on yer property. Why don't you an' yer friends help me get up thar in thet cave an' check it out?'"

"That dog couldn't get from Stringfeller Cavern to that hole up on the cliff," said Mike. "I know caves and I know Stringfeller. That passage would have to drop down a hundred feet or more, go under two streams, then rise back up maybe 200 feet. Can't happen. Didn't happen."

Most of us were cavers of some experience and we knew Mike was right. No way that dog could've gone from Stringfeller to the cliff cave. And now Ralph wants to prove his story was so. And wants us to help him. And, knowing Ralph, probably expected us to do most of the work. Likely all. Damn Ralph and his damn dog.

We sat around belching beer fumes and burger exhaust when it happened.

"You know, I've been thinking . . ." said Ian, "it might be fun. No truth to it, of course, but trying to figure out how to get Ralph's fat ass down in that cave could bring a whole passel of entertainment."

That crazy math teacher. We couldn't believe what Ian was saying. What a great idea! We immediately began throwing ideas around of how to accomplish the task.

"You know, I've been thinking, maybe hammering some pitons, stringing some rope . . ."

"Well, I was thinking maybe shooting a rocket up with a string attached to it and a rope attached to the string, you know . . ."

"I was thinking, 'Hey, how about a weather balloon with a camera to see inside . . .' Nah, on second thought it'd go up too fast even with a guy line."

"Well, what about one of those drones?"

And so it went until Allen had the best idea. "Why don't we let Ralph figure out a way to get down there? As long as he's the one doing it, it'll all be on him. We'll be safe."

"Yeah, but . . ." I said, being the voice of caution by reason of my military career, "you know he's as dumb as a hickory stump. Wouldn't be right unless we were there to at least make sure he doesn't kill himself."

"Okay, Alastair," said Ian, "It will still be a lot of fun." The others seconded that thought.

The next day, we all gathered at the Riverside for breakfast. Bacon, of course, lots of coffee (though Allen was a sissy and drank cream with his), and pancakes. The owner, Edna, made pancakes that were the topic of tales from St. Louis to Little Rock, but these were true tales. Not bald face lies about caves and dogs and such.

As we were sauntering out of the café, Ed got out his mobile phone and called Ralph. He told him to come on over to his place and we'd all take a look at that cliff and the cave where that dog (damn dog) supposedly showed up. It took us about 20 minutes to get back to Ed's.

We were just getting out of the trucks when Ralph raced up Ed's driveway in his green Ford F-150, spraying gravel as he went. This was surprisingly fast for Ralph, who generally took an hour to lift a hand, literally. He jumped out of his truck, hit his head on the door frame on the way out, staggered a second, rubbed his head, knocked off his greasy John Deere hat, stooped to pick it up, banged his head again (on the wing mirror), placed the hat back on his bald pate, straightened up (more or less), and sorta wove his way over to us as though nothing had happened.

"Well, Ah'll be damned, it's the whole dern Derry County brain trust. We'll get this figured out right soon, alright."

Before Ralph got any further, before he started thinking (a thought which sent shivers down our spines), Ed said, "Well, boys, let's take the trucks up to the cliff and check out the situation." After tossing some balding tires and baling wire out of the back of Ralph's truck, and bagged cattle feed out of Ed's, we clambered into the truck beds and held on with white knuckles as Ed and Ralph raced to see who could get over the cattle grate first and on the bumpy track up to the cliff and the cave where Ralph's dog had allegedly showed up. Damn dog.

About 15 minutes later we came to a stop where the track ran out. We shakily climbed out of the trucks and walked over to the base of the cliff.

Now, there needs to be a word or three of explanation about the lay of the land, so to speak. The cliff, as was described earlier, was the former back wall of an enormous cavern which was once situated in the back end of a valley. As one would expect, the cliff was somewhat concave, and its top edge stuck out some 10 feet beyond a small rocky shelf that served as a sort of porch to the cave.

At the base of the cliff was a considerable amount of breakdown, broken rocks and such, caused by the effects of erosion over the centuries since the big cave collapsed. The cliff face itself was made up of limestone and dolomite which was very friable, owing to the same erosion. (We hadn't yet discovered the special hole, it being July and hot and all.)

About 30 feet from the base of the cliff was a fair-sized, spring-fed pond which emptied into a stream which ran alongside the track we rode in on. The pond was relatively deep in places, maybe 15 feet or more in the center. It was hard to tell exactly how deep it was, the water being startlingly clear, and the effect of the light refracting off the surface distorted judgment on those sorts of things. Ed had a problem with Chlorophyta algae in the pond. Because of the strong current of the spring, the algae were clumped together, forming vaguely tree-shaped clusters. To keep this in check, Ed had brought in some grass carp, which wandered around like miniature submarines in and amongst that bright green underwater forest. The carp didn't seem to pay much attention to us, nor did the bass, bluegill, and channel cats that Ed stocked the pond with. However, the bullfrogs and turtles (mostly sliders) took exception to our arrival and promptly plopped their way into their hidey holes.

Up top, near the edge of the cliff, about 15 feet back, an old U.S. Forest Service road, which ran up the gentler slope on the other side, came to an end. The ground up there was fairly stable, the erosion not having eaten that far back.

"Well," observed Ed, "I'm thinking there's no climbing up, even with climbing ropes and pitons. That cliff face is too friable."

"Yeah, and the edge is too far out to rappel onto the shelf in front of the cave," I added. I had some climbing and rappelling experience, and I knew that route was definitely a no-go.

We all turned to Ralph. "Well, Ralph," said Ian, "here's the cave and it was your damn dog. What'cha going to do about this?"

Ralph looked startled at this. He probably figured we'd do all the thinking, us being bright and brainy fellers and all. And, he likely added to his cogitating, if he played his cards right, we'd do all the work as well. Maybe because he had a little smarts in him after all, but more likely to stall off having to do any work, he offered, "Maybe we oughta drive up the Forest Service road and getta view from the top."

We sauntered down to the trucks, climbed aboard, and settled in as best we could for the bone shaking ride up to the top. We finally arrived and stopped in a spray of gravel and pine needles, Ralph a might too close to the edge for our comfort.

We walked over to about two feet from the edge and looked down. I got down on my hands and knees and edged up the last couple of feet, lay flat on my belly, leaned over a bit, and gave the cliff and the shelf a careful examination. I was soon joined by Ed, Ian, and, surprisingly, Ralph. I guess he was excited with the anticipation that we might prove his story was true after all.

"Nope, like I said, there's no rappelling to the shelf, can't even see much of it at all," I said, thoughtfully.

Ed and Ian agreed with me. We edged back away from the lip of the cliff, stood up, dusted off our hands, shirts, and jeans, and headed toward the trucks.

We expected Ralph was following us, but when we joined a meeting in progress around Ed's Chevy, we looked around. There was Ralph, still back at the cliff. He returned to the rest of us, shaking his head sadly. Then he stopped suddenly. He spied a stack of shortleaf pine logs, about 50 feet in length and a foot in diameter, lying beside the road. The Forest Service had been doing some select cutting and stacked the results of their work just to the other side of the road from us.

Ralph walked over to the logs and stood there silently. Suddenly, he got a glint in his eyes, and we all started worrying. Ralph was thinking. He should know better than that—he should leave it to us professional thinkers.

"Yah know, I'm thinkin' we could cleat a couple of them thar logs together, maybe overlap 'em around three feet. Nail some rungs on 'em, build a kinda ladder. Then we could loop a short chain around one end, fix the chain up close to the tail hitch of a truck, and back 'er up slow an' lower the other end over the edge till it touched down, an' climb down at least close enough to look into the cave. Maybe even be able to swing in thar with a rope."

Well, why not? We didn't have any better ideas. Besides, even though Ralph might not know it, he was the one who was going to be doing the climbing. It was his damn dog.

Ed got a couple of log lifters with steel cant hooks from under a tarp in the back of his truck. ("I wondered what I had been sitting on," mused Allen.) Together with these and some come-alongs, we positioned the logs and cleated them together with some long spikes Ed produced out from behind the driver's seat and a small sledge from his toolbox (the same sledge Steve would use later). We fashioned some rungs out of smaller logs we found nearby using a chainsaw and a splitting maul Ralph had in his truck. We positioned the makeshift ladder behind Ralph's truck and chained it up as he described.

Ralph complained, "Why my truck?"

"Because it was your idea," we all chimed in unison.

Ralph made sure the four-wheel drive hubs were locked and climbed in behind the steering wheel, started up his truck which promptly belched out a black cloud of oil ladened smoke. Why hadn't we noticed that earlier?

"Truck's not much good," observed Allen.

"Yeah, and I wonder how good his brakes are, might need 'em," added Steve.

Ralph shifted into reverse and began to slowly edge toward the cliff.

Ian got a worried look on his face. "How much you reckon that truck of his weighs, Ed?"

"Oh, I should imagine about two and a half tons."

Both Ian and Ed looked at each other, looked at Ralph backing up his truck, the log going back with it in a kind of wig-wagging manner.

"Ralph, wait!" Ed and Ian shouted. We all joined in, but he couldn't hear us over the noise of his engine's belching and coughing. We ran toward him, waving our arms, but he was looking to the rear and never saw us.

After the ladder hung about 10 feet over the edge, it began to exert some leverage on the truck, kinda lifting it in short bumps. Ralph was looking worried. In another 10 feet the truck began to slide. Ralph stomped on the breaks. We soon found out the answer to Steve's question: not very good at all. He then shifted into first, but all that did was send a shower of gravel and pine needles back toward the cliff edge. When he realized he wasn't going to halt the ladder's and the truck's steady progress, he jumped out of the cab, only to see the ladder slide over the edge, catch on a rock for a brief moment, and slingshot the truck over the lip of the cliff. We heard a series of loud crashes and a single, tremendous splash.

We walked carefully over to the edge and looked down in time to see Ralph's F-150 settle slowly into the depths of the pond, releasing wave after wave of bubbles as it went. It spooked the fish something bad. Even the grass carp began looking for a way to escape down the stream exiting the pond.

Ed and Ian took a quivering, babbling Ralph by the arms over to Ed's truck and settled him in the passenger seat. Ian climbed into the back. Ed drove off slowly, leaving the rest of us standing by the edge, watching in stunned amazement as that green F-150 settled into the algae forest, blending in as if it were just one more Chlorophyta "tree."

When we turned around, we realized Ed left without us. So, we walked silently down the Forest Service road. It took us about an hour. When we got to where the road joined the gravel drive to Ed's place, Steve's shoulders began to shake. We thought he was crying, and we gathered around him. Then we noticed: Steve was laughing. At first, we thought he was being highly insensitive, what with him being a psychologist and all. But soon we joined in with him.

"Did you see that truck? Flew through the air like it had been launched by a trebuchet!"[2] Steve choked out between barks of laughter.

"And did you see Ralph's face when his brakes failed?" Allen added.

"And when he scrambled out of that truck?" giggled Mike.

"Poor Ralph," I said, before breaking out into another fit of mirth. Tears were streaming down our faces, and we were hanging on to each other to steady ourselves as we walked the last hundred yards up to Ed's house.

---

[2] A medieval siege machine, like a catapult, but which used a heavy counterbalance instead of tension to launch its missile.

When we arrived, Ralph was sitting under a tree next to the house with a dazed expression on his face. Occasionally he would take a sip of beer from a can some thoughtful soul had given him, hiccup, and return to his sorrows. We composed ourselves as best we could, wiping our streaming faces with the backs of our hands.

Ed and Ian were standing at the front of Ed's Chevy, heads together in quiet conversation. When we joined them, we saw they were scribbling some numbers on a scrap from a paper feed bag.

"So, you say the truck weighed how much? And how much do you reckon that ladder weighed? And it was what, nearly 100 feet long?" They did some more scribbling.

Ian looked up, saw us, and said, "Well, as near as Ed and I can figure it, that ladder acted like a lever exerting over 50,000 foot-pounds of energy. Ralph's truck, being around 5,000 pounds, didn't stand a chance."

Ed nodded. "Threw his truck clean into the pond like it was a trebuchet."

"We couldn't do the math," Steve responded, "but that's about how we figured it."

We stood around thoughtfully, and then the laughter came again, and this time Ed and Ian joined in. We tried to control ourselves, out of courtesy to Ralph, but he was beyond knowing or even caring.

Ed stopped. "You know, I've been thinking, how am I going to get his truck out of the pond?" he asked to no one in particular.

"You know, I've been thinking, better do the math beforehand this time," I observed.

We broke out into laughter once more.

Ralph's truck was eventually hauled out of the pond. We got in a canoe which Ed kept lying nearby. We carried a cable with a hook and snagged it on to the chain attached to the floating makeshift ladder, and a Forest Service bulldozer, thoughtfully lent to us by a friend of Mike, pulled the truck out without too much problem.

Later, we got a very tall extension ladder from some painter friends of Steve, rested it against the base of the cliff, anchoring it with a chain to a boulder. It just reached the edge of the rocky shelf in front of the cave. We gingerly climbed up, one at a time, and hauled up some caving equipment, lights, helmets, and such. We geared up and made our way into the cave. It was sandy and dry and only ran about 50 feet before it petered out. No connection to Stringfeller. No way that dog could have come out here. Damn dog.

Homemade Artillery and Its Effect on Cows

During the University summer break a couple of years ago, I drove up from Little Rock to visit my Ozark mad scientist friends. I pulled up in front of Ed's place in my Prius (yeah, I'm one of those "lib'rals," but hey, I'm a college dean, after all) and joined a meeting in progress at the tailgate of Ed's truck. Standing there were Ed, Mike, and Allen. They were looking at a large piece of PVC pipe, around 12 inches in diameter, strapped to a utility trailer hitched to the truck. It was clear they were thinking. "Oh no," I thought. "What now?"

I heard just a snippet of their conversation and I realized they were discussing building the largest homemade canon in Derry County history, maybe even in all the Ozarks. This was crazy! Ridiculous! I knew this was going to be fun.

I should give some background. Last Fall, Ed read an article online about potato guns. For those of you who don't know, these pieces of makeshift artillery are made by taking a four-foot-long piece of heavy PVC pipe, about three inches or so in diameter, and sealing up one end with a PVC cap glued in place with some plumber's glue. A hole would be drilled into the end near the cap and the business end of a fireplace lighter would be inserted into the hole. You would then spray some sort of propellant, usually hairspray, into the pipe, ram in a potato, and ignite the lighter. The potato would explode out of the pipe and strike some unsuspecting target, hopefully not some unsuspecting animal or person, but you never knew. The boom of the exploding fuel and the follow-up thwack of the potato's untimely demise were very satisfying. Especially to mountain mad scientists.

But Ed wasn't satisfied with such a small caliber cannon, and he began upgrading his arsenal. He continued enlarging his guns and increasing the amount of propellant until he was able to shoot two-liter Coke bottles some 100 or more yards away. He discovered you could do a lot of damage if you filled the bottle maybe three-quarters full (to allow for expansion) with water, let it freeze overnight, and then fire the projectile at some appropriate target. Ed mainly went after the Osage orange and locust trees which had invaded his fence rows, snapping them over with a gratifying Bang! Snap! Crack! Occasionally, he'd instead hit the fence and the barbed wire, which was under some considerable tension, would pull three or four fence posts out of the ground and fling them in the air, before breaking free of the wire staples and returning to its more-or-less original position with an echoing Thwang! like the release of an enormous bowstring.

When Ed was about half-way through explaining the technical details of the project, we heard the crunch of gravel and turned to see our friend, Jimmy, driving his Dodge Caravan (complete with faux wood paneling—even less manly than my Prius) up into the yard. Jimmy (short for Jameson) was an old friend from my Navy days when I was assigned to the

Pentagon who now lived in St. Louis. I had invited him down to go floating on the Greystone River three years back, and I introduced him to my friends in Derry County. He fell in love with the Ozarks, enjoyed his time with my crazy, over-educated friends, and couldn't wait to get away from work and join us on our adventures in mountain mad science.

Jimmy was a computer geek who worked for the government. He wouldn't tell us what part of the government (or even which government for that matter). We happily accepted him into our group, even though he was from northern Illinois, because he brought a special skill to our informal club: Jimmy knew how to blow up things. You see, Jimmy had been in the Air Force for a while and dropped bombs from a B-52. He blew up a lot of things in both Gulf Wars. Perfect addition to our gang.

"Hey, guys," said Jimmy, in his slightly nasal twang and flat vowels, which sounded all the more jarring because of his baritone voice. Well, we can't all be perfect.

"Hey yourself, Jimmy," replied Ed laconically. But Ed and, indeed, all of us were glad to see him. Here we were talking about artillery, trajectories, explosive yields, and damage projections: Jimmy would fit right in. Hell, he'd be the resident (albeit temporary) expert.

For Jimmy's benefit, Ed started all over from the beginning. The way he told it, it seems the Derry County Highway Department, including its Director, Earl, in his yellow county pickup truck, a yellow county dump truck (with its driver) with a utility trailer, a yellow frontend loader/backhoe (with its operator), and a pick and shovel (with their dual-certified technician)—in other words, the entire Highway Department—were slipping pipes into the culverts underneath the low-water bridge on Locust Creek. The culverts were rusting out, and, rather than dig them out, they were inserting 12-inch diameter six-foot long PVC pipes in each culvert and concreting each end to seal them up tight around the corroding steel. These were big, heavy-duty jobs, light green in color, with the sleeve walls about an inch and a quarter thick. One of the pipes had a broken collar (where one pipe slipped into another), and such was the damage that it couldn't be used.

Ed was just going to pass these boys by with a wave and a beep. But then he saw that broken pipe, and with it came a vision in which the world went into slow motion. The realization of what that pipe could be used for. The magnificence of its larger caliber. The possession of a gun that could inspire the gravest envy and, frankly, a Freudian lust. The understanding that these guys couldn't use the pipe. And, oh joy of joys, it looked like they were packing it up for the day. All these swirled simultaneously around the finely tuned brain lobes of this retired physics professor. He must act.

His truck skidded to a stop alongside Earl's pickup. Earl was leaning against the closed driver's side door with a distracted look on his face. Ed rolled down his window. "Say, Earl," said Ed to the Director, "are you boys gonna use that piece of broken pipe?" He tried to speak in a matter-of-fact tone. He was afraid if he awoke Earl's suspicions that the pipe would be horribly transported from the roadside to the dump truck to the junk pile at the County Highway Department depot, from whence nothing ever, ever departed. The pile was a good 30 feet high at the time of Ed's story. It would only grow higher.

Earl looked at Ed. He started to get suspicious. He knew Ed's reputation. He remembered back when Ed was a lowly physics teacher at Providence High School and how he blew out the power because of one of his experiments. Not just in the high school. Not just in Providence. Not just in Derry

County. The whole darn grid went down in Derry, Bean, and the western half of Rhett counties.

He started to say, "You cain't take it, Ed, gotta take this back to the depot." But then he saw that the boys had attached the utility trailer to the dump truck and were fixing to drive the frontend loader/backhoe up the ramps onto the trailer. He saw the technician had already thrown the pick and shovel into the dump truck and was climbing into the dump truck cab. He looked at his watch and saw it was 4:30. By the time the boys got finished with what they were doing, stretch and scratch, listened to and questioned the instructions about the pipe, stretch and scratch, figured out the best way to move the pipe into the dump truck, determined the best location for the pipe to lie, stretch and scratch, picked up the pipe, lifted it up into the bed of the dump truck, stretch and scratch, and got into the trucks and drove to the depot, it would easily be 5:30, if not later. The County Commissioners were already breathing down his neck about overtime. If they left right now, they could make it by 5:00.

Earl gave Ed a world-weary, what's-a-poor-county-official-gonna-do look, and said, "It's broke, Ed. Cain't use it. You can take it if you want to."

That's all he needed to hear. "Okay, Earl, leave it here. I'll be back for it right away."

"Alright, fine."

Earl got in his truck, started it, and honked the horn to let the driver, operator, and technician know it was past time to get a move on. Simultaneously, Ed disappeared in a cloud of dust and air-suspended gravel.

About 20 minutes later, with the help of his own utility trailer, a come-along, and a canvas strap, Ed was happily returning home, the proud owner of one future 12-inch gun.

So now there we were, silently gathered around the pipe, dreaming dreams and seeing visions, as the Prophet Joel once said. Then it started.

"You know, I'm thinking it'd take a whole case of hair spray to use as fuel for this baby."

"Yeah, and I'm thinking what're we gonna use as ammunition?"

"And I've been thinking, that thing goes off, it could blow off somebody's head. Gotta find some way to secure it without holding it by hand."

That last observation, coming from me, sobered us up a bit. Typically, a potato gun is fired from the shoulder, like a bazooka, or from the hip, like a shotgun in an old-fashioned Western. The coke-bottle gun was just sort of wedged in the bed of Ed's Chevy, between the side wall and a sack or two of cattle feed. Obviously, none of these were viable options for this caliber of a gun.

"Well, it could be fired like a mortar."

We all turned to the speaker. Jimmy, delivering the goods on all things explosive.

"Yeah, we could dig a small hole to put the butt end in, make a stand out of a couple of pieces of steel pipe welded together. Should be good," he added.

Ed's, Mike's, and Allen's eyes all lit up. The possibilities were enormous. Then a question:

"What about propellent?" asked Mike.

"That's easy. We drill a hole down by the butt end, insert a brass nozzle, glue it in place, and attach an LP bottle by a supply hose," Jimmy replied.

"But" persisted Mike, "that much gas, it'll need additional air in order to ignite."

Jimmy shrugged off the problem. "Put in another nozzle and attach a line from a compressed air tank. I see Ed's got one in his truck bed."

"And we can use the same kind of ignition, right? A fireplace lighter?" Allen asked.

"Umm," I interjected quietly. "Who's gonna stand by that darn mortar and pull the trigger? Sounds pretty risky to me."

The sudden silence showed they all saw the point.

Then Jimmy brightened and said, "We'll use an electric ignition switch. Easy. Hook up two leads to a 12-volt battery, splice in a simple throw switch on one of them and bore two small holes for the wires. Flip the switch, sparks fly, BOOM!"

Amazing! Shear genius. It's a wonder Jimmy didn't blow up the whole darn Middle East.

One last question. "And ammunition?" asked Mike.

"Well, I've been thinking," said Ed, "I've got some watermelons back at the house."

We looked at one another, stunned at the audacity. Of course! What better? It was the perfect projectile for the 12-inch barrel. Sure, it'd need a little shaving here and there to get it to fit. Afterall, no watermelon is perfect. Easy fix.

A few hours later, we were all set. After an operational meeting in which possible test locations were discussed, it was decided to go to the large field down where Ed had been pasturing some of his cattle.

I need to take another pause and talk about that field and its adjacent features. The field was a fine pasture, with thick green grass even during the hottest summer. The reason for that was Low Wassie Spring, the outflow of which, Low Wassie Creek, meandered through the middle of the field, joining Locust Creek down close to the low-water bridge I mentioned earlier. (I never heard tell of a High Wassie, by the way. Low Wassie is probably a corruption of "low water.")

Low Wassie Spring put out a fair bit of water. Nothing anywhere near comparable to nearby Goliath Springs with its 3,000 gallons of water per second, making it the main source of the Greystone River and one of the four largest springs in the Ozarks. This spring? Probably only around 16 gallons or so.

The spring entered the field at its northwest corner from Low Wassie Cave. The cave was a good 25 or so feet across most of its length, the spring's bed occupying anywhere from a quarter to the full extent of the cave's one and only passage. It varied between six inches to a couple of feet deep. It only extended back into the hill about 50 yards, more or less, swooping in a broad, S-shaped curve toward the back where the spring emerged from the rock wall.

Flooding down on the Locust would often cause some back flow from the creek and that, combined with how low and relatively level the pasture was, caused an area, which extended from about 50 feet in front of the cave entrance to about another 50 feet inside the cave, to lie with about a foot of mud most of the year.

Ed's cows liked that mud. They would sort of wallow around in it and cover themselves with its sticky, red clay goo. It protected the cattle well from mosquitos and flies, though when it dried it gave the beasts a rather grisly, blood-flecked appearance, as though they had been disappointingly close to a mass murder.

The cows also like the cool interior of the cave and spent their time resting there out of the sun. That summer, the weather was unusually warm.

Meanwhile, back at Ed's place, we gathered up our supplies and piled into the cab and truck bed of his Chevy and headed out to the field. It was a large field, plenty of clear open space. No way we could hit something accidentally. Well, just goes to show.

We arrived at the field, opened a gate, and the five of us man-handled the mortar in position. We dug the shallow hole and set up a frame. Turns out we didn't have to weld one. Ed found the perfect thing in his barn: a large, metal triangle with a little V-shaped projection welded at one of the vertices.

"Have no idea what this is for," remarked Ed, when he found it. We never did discover its purpose.

We set up the tube, carefully grounding the butt end and cradling the business end in the stand. We attached the leads and hoses, wired in the switch, set up the LP and air tanks, connected the battery, and inserted the ammo. The last was a little tight, but better seal, better pressure, better BOOM!

"How much gas and air do you suppose?" asked Ed, looking at Jimmy.

"Hell, I don't know. Probably should have put some gages on to measure it. Let's just check it out now, and we can add them later."

Ed nodded. He turned on the valves to the air and gas tanks, let them fill the tube for a few seconds, and looked around inquiringly.

"Probably ought to add some more," said Mike.

Ed did so.

"How do we know we got the air-fuel mixture right?" I asked.

Ed shrugged. "I have no idea. I guess we'll find out."

We stood about 10 feet back from the mortar and put on goggles and inserted ear plugs. Hey, safety first, right?

Ed threw the switch. There was a loud boom. An enormous flash. A reverberating echo. Sudden silence.

Now, I'm sure the cow that wandered out of Low Wassie Cave at that moment, after a satisfying mud bath, had no idea that Ed and his crew of mountain mad scientists were set up on the southeast corner of the field. I'm also sure the cow had no idea about the light green colored PVC pipe, or the various hoses and wires attached thereto. Nor did she know of the specially sculpted melon. It's a pretty safe bet she had no appreciation for the inventiveness of that piece of artillery.

In any event, just as she wandered out of the cave, she heard the gun's report, sensed impending danger, and looked up. Quite suddenly, to her great surprise and consternation, a watermelon exploded. On her head. She cocked that head to one side, as though she developed a sudden and substantial crick in her neck, turned around, and wobbled back into the cave.

We saw the whole thing. We gasped in disbelief as the watermelon detonated on the cow's head, covering her with a red, sloppy sludge, which, added to the red clay mud, made her look like a victim in a B-movie. We were astonished that she didn't fall over dead. We were further astounded when she wobbled back toward the opening, disappearing into the darkness and, she probably hoped, the safety of Low Wassie Cave.

"I can't believe that watermelon flew that far," said Mike, shaking his head. "Musta been a hundred yards."

"I can't believe the barrel is still intact," marveled Allen. "I can't believe that cow is still alive," said a thoroughly amazed Ed.

"I'm thinking," I mused, "we probably should have installed those gages."

"Why?" asked Jimmy, "it worked, didn't it?"

"Yeah, too well. Need to dial it back a notch or two," I answered.

A couple of months later, I was talking to Jimmy on the phone. He and his wife, Helen, were planning on visiting my wife, Elsbeth, and me in Little Rock, and Jimmy and I were working some details.

"By the way," Jimmy said, "I was talking to Ed the other day."

"Oh?"

"Yeah, and I asked him about the cow."

"The one he exploded the watermelon on its head?"

"The very one. Anyhow, he says that when the cow starts to come out of the cave, it stops at the edge of the opening and looks around. If Ed's in sight, the cow turns around and goes back inside."

"Good memory for a cow."

"Yeah, sure is." He paused a moment. "Alastair, you know, Ed says that cow's head is still bent to the side. Looks comically quizzical all the time, as if it's still wondering what happened."

"I know what happened."

"What do you mean, other than the obvious?"

"This is what happens when you get a bunch of Ozarkans with graduate degrees together with nothing better to do."

"Yeah, probably right," he said in his flat northern Illinois accent. "Funny though." He chuckled. I joined him.

Hey, Jimmy's from Illinois, but he's a for-sure mountain mad scientist like the rest of us.

Pig Fences May Fly

"It's iniquitous, that's what it is, iniquitous!"

We looked up, startled, as Mike came tromping over to our regular table at the Riverside. Disturbing our coffee, pancakes, and bacon, he'd better have a darn good reason for this noisy, digestion-interrupting commotion.

"What's the problem, Mike?" asked Allen.

"The cost of hog-proof fencing, that's what! It's going to cost me a small fortune to fence that pig pasture! It's . . ."

"Iniquitous," we agreed in a monotone chorus, with only a hint of annoyance.

Mike was a biologist for the Missouri Department of Conservation. He made good money at his job, but his wife, Nora, wanted to do some extensive remodeling to their house, like replacing the avocado green kitchen appliances and pink bathroom fixtures.

"Nora, that stove works perfectly well," said Mike, finishing his coffee.

"Mike, it's from 1973 when the house was built," Nora retorted.

"So? I was born in 1963 and I'm doing just fine." Mike stood up from the table with a series of muffled creaks and cracks coming from his back. He rubbed his left shoulder, still sore from washing his state-supplied pickup.

"Yeah, right, just like your shoulder works fine. Who hurts their shoulder while washing their truck? I'll tell you who—old men do—and you're getting old."

Mike looked pained for a moment, as much from the verbal gut-punch from Nora as from his back and shoulders. He started to reply but Nora cut him off.

"I'm sorry, I shouldn't have said you're old. But, Mike, only three of the four burners of the stove work right. The other has only one temp, regardless of what setting you put it on: flash char. And we're constantly having to get the fridge fixed. Last month it was a new compressor. We've put enough money into that thing to have bought two new ones by now. The dishwasher hasn't worked in ages."

"We've got a perfectly good dishwasher, three actually—the kids."

"Ha, ha. I've got news for you. The twins are starting high school next year and they're going to be so busy with band and sports and clubs we won't hardly see them. And MJ is not too far behind. Are you going to take over for them?" (MJ is Mike Junior and the twins are Ellen and Maggie.)

"Err," replied Mike.

"And don't even get me started on the master bath. To flush the toilet, you have to stand there holding the handle down for a good minute and a half and, Mike, sometimes you don't hold the handle down long enough."

"Well, okay, we'll replace the toilet, but everything else works okay."

"Mike, I'm not having a 1970s Pepto-Bismol pink bathtub and sink and tiles and a white toilet. We're getting a new kitchen and a new master bath and then we're going to start looking at the other bathroom as well."

"Eep," was all Mike could say.

One Saturday morning, while Nora and the kids were out, Mike sat down at the kitchen table and started to consider his options. His job had him working 50 or more hours a week, much of it outdoors and pretty physical. He didn't think he could handle a part-time job on top of this, even one of those work-from-home gimmicks that he was seeing on the TV. Nora was splitting her days between working as a part-time visiting nurse, sharing the care of her invalid mother with her sister, and riding herd on MJ, Ellen, Maggie, and Mike. That's about two full-time jobs worth of effort, reflected Mike.

He thought, "What else do I have so I can make some money?" There was the five-acre field across the road from the house. He had been renting the field out to Ed to pasture a few cattle in, but Ed cleared another pasture up by the oxbow lake on his property, and he didn't need Mike's land. So, no go. Besides, Mike really didn't want to take on farming, even on a small scale—too much work.

And then it happened: Mike started thinking. He remembered attending a meeting of folks from some state and county agencies. A speaker from the University of Missouri Extension Service gave a talk on pasturing pigs. Instead of keeping them in a feedlot, constantly feeding them, and slopping the pen out, you fenced off some acreage with good pig fencing, used a seed drill to plant pig pasture mix (turnips, alfalfa, rapeseed, and such), made sure they had a good water supply, and beyond some routine maintenance and hauling the pigs off to be slaughtered, that was pretty much it. If you had a good pasture, you could raise 25 hogs on a single acre.

Mike reached over and grabbed a pen and some note paper that were by the kitchen phone. He started to do some figuring. "Let's see, there's a part of the field that backs against some oak trees—acorns are good for pigs. That's maybe the size of a football field, say maybe one and a quarter acre. Now that'd be around 360 feet by 160 feet. If I crossed-fenced it, let's say twice, to move the pigs around and keep erosion down, that'd be, let's see . . ." He did some quick math. "That'd be about 1,360 feet. I'd have to put in three heavy-duty gates. And fenceposts, they'd have to be heavy-duty as well, say every eight feet." He did some more math. "That's 170 posts. Oh, I'd have to open up that old well, install a pump, and set up a stock tank pool in each section. Wow, this could run into some money." He picked up the sheet of scratch paper, folded it, and put it in his pocket. He walked out to his truck, grabbing his hat and keys on the way, and headed to Providence Feed and Supply.

Providence Feed and Supply was an old-fashioned business where customers walked up to the counter and told an employee what they needed. You described a project; they would grab a legal pad and start writing the "grocery list" as well the prices for each item. It was seldom the case that any of the store clerks ever had to look up the price on anything.

"Let's see, Mike." Seemed like the staff knew everyone in Derry County. "That's 1,360 feet of hog fencing, 170 posts and three spools of fencing wire to attach the fencing, three heavy bar gates, three stock pools, a pump, and heavy-duty hose. You're looking at . . ." He crunched the numbers. He showed them to Mike. Mike gulped. He thanked the clerk for his time.

"Sure 'nuff, Mike, any time. Let me know if you want me to order it."

"Err," replied Mike. "Ahh, well . . ."

Mike climbed back into the truck and headed home. He searched his mind for the right word to describe the situation. Expensive? Pah! A sickly word, a worm-like word, not worth the merest consideration. Usurious? Better, getting there, had a bit more punch. Iniquitous? Yes! Iniquitous! It sounded all King James-esque, all thunder-and-lightening-on-Mount-Sinai, and right now a good Bible word, one redolent of divine wrath and holy disapprobation, was just what he needed. Iniquitous!

He changed his mind about going back to the house, did a U-turn back toward town, pulled up into the parking lot of the Riverside, banged through the front door, and interrupted our late and leisurely Saturday breakfast. He filled us in on the situation, including Nora's plans and the pig pasture.

"And it's going to cost $12,566 plus tax! Iniquitous, I tell you, I-N-I, ah, C, no, Q, oh never mind! Iniquitous!" I guess you don't have to spell Bible words to be a successful state biologist.

"There's no way Nora's gonna let you spend that. And are you sure you want to take on pasturing pigs?" I asked.

"Yeah, the university extension guy said it was pretty easy. And there's a good market right now for organic, pasture-fed pork," replied Mike.

Ed shook his head. "Mike, I was at the same meeting as you, and I think you're forgetting something he said, something like, 'After an initial investment, which can, I admit, be expensive, the cost of raising pasture-fed pigs is pretty low.' I also seem to remember him saying it would be three to four years before you recoup your investment."

"And" Allen added, who raised pasture-fed pigs himself, "you still have to buy supplemental feed to increase the protein in their diet. Organic feed's pretty high."

Mike sat glumly considering the untimely demise of a brilliant idea.

"You know, I'm thinking," I said, "the really big upfront expense is the fencing. Is there any way to buy used fencing? You know, maybe some farmer decided he's getting out of the livestock pasturing business or maybe he's going to sell out to a housing developer. Lot of folks moving here from Kansas City and St. Louis since they can work from home over the internet."

"Yeah, that's right," said Steve. "Ever since Century-Tel put in that new fiberoptic system, internet's been pretty good. I've started doing some consulting work from home."

"So," Mike said, reflectively, "Who do we know who's got some fence he'd be willing to part with?" We all looked blankly at one another.

I stood up to go pay my bill. "Hey, let's keep an eye out this week and see if we can find leads. I'm heading back to Little Rock next week, but in the meantime, I'll ask around."

"Better find something soon or Nora's gonna have me working at the Kwik-Mart on Saturdays and Sundays."

Since I was spending the week canoeing and hiking with Elsbeth, I didn't see a lot of the locals. Just some teenagers at the canoe rental place and an exhausted single mom working the register at the Super Save. On my last day in town, I went into the Mercantile to say goodbye to Bat Simmons. As I turned to leave, a thought occurred to me, and I returned to the front counter behind which Bat sat on a high stool to survey his "kingdom."

"Say, Mr. Simmons, you know most of what goes on around here—you heard of anyone selling their land, or maybe deciding to stop farming, and they got a lot of fencing they might let go of, cheap?"

Bat scratched his head, thoughtfully. "Don't most folks sell their fence. Jist let the posts and the wire rust away or, iff'n they do sell their land to some devel'pers, they jist bulldoze the post down up into a burn pile 'n burn it with the brush from clearin' the land. Maybe haul off the bits of wire to the dump, but more likely jist bury 'em."

"Yeah, that's about what I thought," I said. "But if anybody comes to mind, let Mike know."

"Will do. Have a safe trip back to Little Rock, Alastair."

"See you in a few months, Mr. Simmons." I waved and left the store, the little brass bell set on the door jingling good-bye.

A couple of months later, I got a call from Ed asking me if I was still in the market for some of his grass-fed beef. He was proud of his herd, and he was careful to manage the pastures and the quality of the drinking water. Even when he supplemented their diet during the winter or when finishing them up before slaughter, he used only organic high protein feed. No antibiotics, no bovine growth hormone. Ed reasoned that, if you kept cattle in an environment as close to the steppes of their ancestors as possible, you'd have healthy cows that produced good quality meat. So far, his herd was proving him right.

"Sure," I said. "Put me down for just a quarter this time. I still have some left from the half I ordered last time."

"Will do," Ed replied. He quoted me a price and I indicated that would be fine.

"Say," said Ed. "I think I can get this butchered and packaged by the weekend after next. Why don't you come on up and maybe we can get some time on the river? You can stay in the guest room."

"Sounds good to me. Elsbeth's babysitting the grandkids at their house that weekend. I can get away, yeah, no problem."

"Okay, see you then."

As I hung up the phone, I had visions of steaks cooking on the grill (you had to marinate them because they were so lean), chili super-loaded with ground beef, and pot roasts for Sunday dinner. All tasty and, unlike feedlot beef, all good for you.

Then my thoughts quickly turned to the Greystone, the mist lifting off the river as the sun rose, the blue-green water dazzling in the open spaces then turning dark and mysterious as it slipped under some overhanging sycamores. I remembered the music of the river and, meat or no, I knew I had to go back to Derry County once more.

One weekend passed and the following Friday came. I packed up a borrowed pickup with the usual kit for a weekend visit to my friends, some fishing gear (I hoped to tangle with some of those new hybrid brown trout), and three large ice chests for the meat. The trip up US 67 to Oakmont, where I stayed with my mom, was uneventful. The next day, before sunup, I headed over to Ed's place in Derry County.

Traveling through the eastern foothills then the ridge-and-valley regions of the eastern Ozarks was a tonic for my soul. We were trying to get accreditation for the College of

Education's new master's degree in STEM education and the accreditors were being, I thought, quite unreasonable in how we were going to measure outcomes. I knew I would have to give-in on this but still . . . I needed a good dose of Derry County.

I didn't take my usual route through downtown Providence—I knew if I did, about a half dozen people would want me to stop and spend some time "yarnin'." Instead, I took the new highway to the south of the town which led to the county road that went up to Ed's farm. Pulling off the road onto the gravel drive, I saw Ed, together with Mike and Ian, standing around some contraption chained down to a trailer hitched behind Mike's state government truck. It had hoses, wires, and gauges, and what for all the world looked like a giant metal syringe. I was pretty sure there wouldn't be any canoeing on the Greystone, at least not today.

The guys waved at me as I pulled up. Getting out of the truck, I walked over to the three. Ed and Mike were talking excitedly while Ian was standing with his arms folded, shaking his head. I was worried. I could tell Ed and Mike had been thinking, and Ian thought whatever they came up with was a bad idea. If even Ian thought it was a no go, then it had to be stupid, dangerous, or both. Ian's rate of head shaking said, "It's both."

Ed turned toward me. "Hey, Alastair. Good to see you. Is that your truck?" Ed was not a religious man, but he lived in the fervent hope that our crazy bomber friend, Jimmy, and I would both see reason and get rid of Jimmy's Dodge Caravan and my Prius and buy respectable pickup trucks. Preferably Chevies, but Ed wasn't picky.

"Nah, Ed, just borrowed it for the weekend to come get the meat," I replied. "Um, what's up guys? Are we gonna float the river today?"

"Sorry, Alastair, not today, but we can get on the river tomorrow if you have the time. I shoulda called you."

"Well, I can manage a short, half-day float, but I gotta get on the road tomorrow afternoon. I've got a meeting with the accreditors about our new STEM program. You know what that's like."

Ed nodded in disgust. As a retired physics professor from Missouri State, he did indeed know what that's like.

I was pretty disappointed because I knew there would not be much of a chance for fishing tomorrow, but my scientific curiosity about that machine was a sufficient enough distraction to cause me to be "present in the moment" (psychobabble from my colleagues down the hall in the Behavioral Science Department, but it seemed appropriate for this instance).

"What's going on, guys? And what's this contraption all about?" I asked.

Mike got an enormous, face-splitting grin on his face. Oh, no.

"Well, Alastair, it's like this," said Mike, in a tone that sounded a good deal like dangerous enthusiasm. I could tell by the look on Ian's face that he and I were of the same mind.

The week before last, shortly after Ed and I had talked, Bat Simmons called Mike. Ralph MacKay's brother, Titus, was in the Mercantile that morning. He told Bat that he was turning one of his large cow pastures, which ran a considerable distance along the banks of the Greystone, into an RV park. Bat knew that piece of property and also knew that, in a fit of rare industry, Titus had installed some heavy fencing to keep the cows out of the river, the bank there being pretty steep and clayey.

Bat told Titus that Mike was looking for some fencing like his and wondered if it'd be okay for Mike to come get it.

"Sure," Titus had said. "Ah was jist gonna bulldoze 'em along with some trees that'd blowed down in that dern storm last week and light 'em up. He kin have what he wants."

Bat thanked him, and, as Titus left the store, he called Mike and told him the good news.

The next day, Mike showed up at Titus's field with the back end of his state-owned pickup truck full of sundry tools and equipment. He somehow managed to talk Ed into lending a hand. Ed was dubious at first but realized he might be able to get some fishing in—some of those hybrid brown trout were caught near there recently. Since it was a catch-and-release stretch of the river, there was a good chance they'd still be there. So, he agreed.

They got out of the truck and walked over to the fence. The fencing was perfect—just some superficial rust here and there, otherwise the zinc coating held up pretty well. The posts looked good too.

"You know, Mike, if we got only half of this fence and the posts, that'd be all you need. Man, that'd save you some money," Ed observed.

"Yeah, a *lot* of money," agreed Mike, and he went eagerly back to the pickup and started unloading some of the gear. Mike grabbed a pick and shovel, and Ed snagged a couple of pairs of leather work gloves and a toolbox from the truck cab. They sauntered over to a gate.

"You reckon Titus'll let us take the gates too?" Mike asked, his eyes glittering with hope.

"Don't see why not," replied Ed.

Mike flashed an enormous smile. "Man, that's even more money that stays in the bank. Nora's going to be happy about this."

They took down the gate so that they had a free end of the fence to start on. They turned their attention to the first post. It was a typical steel post, with a green, enamel-like coating for most of its length, topped with a white cap. It was set pretty firmly in the red clay. After cutting the fence ties free from the post, Mike pushed and pulled on it a couple of times to see if it could be wiggled out. He didn't have much hope that'd work, but you never knew. The post didn't budge. He and Ed worked together, trying to seesaw the post loose. Nothing. Pretty firmly set indeed.

Next, they used the pick and shovel to try and loosen up the ground around the post. The pick bounced off the hard-packed, sunbaked clay and the shovel's blade came to a jarring halt within a quarter of an inch below the surface. The clay was not cooperating with Mike's desire to become a pig farmer and he was becoming frustrated. It being the tail-end of summer, he should have known that packed red clay would be about as hard as rock.

Mike and Ed returned to the truck and got out a heavy steel, three-legged frame, which they erected over the fence post. After a few more trips, they had a block and tackle assembly set up, ready for action. Mike took a length of chain and wrapped it around the post and used a hook to hold the chain in place. He then connected the other end to the pulley. Mike pulled down on the haul. Nothing happened. He rubbed his hands on his jeans, got a new hold, and pulled again. Nada. Mike looked over to Ed and jerked his head to signal he should join him. Ed's hands joined Mike's on the haul.

"One, two, three, pull!" chanted Mike.

But after some ten minutes it became clear that all of Mike's chanting and their combined pulling were not going to convince that post to come out of the ground. It was quite content to remain where it was, thank you very much.

They tried on a couple of other posts, with no better results.

"Hell," said Ed. "they are not coming out this way."

Mike nodded glumly. That clay was like concrete. At this rate, they'd have to use a jack hammer. Or dynamite.

Mike let down the tailgate of his truck, sat down on it, and reached behind him to snag some beers out of an ice chest. He retrieved two cans and held one out to Ed. Ed thanked him, took the can, and joined him on the tailgate. There was the sound of two metallic pops followed by prolonged silence, interrupted from time to time by the slurping of beer. Mike and Ed sat there, thinking.

Suddenly Mike's eyes lit up. "Say, Ed."

"Yeah?"

"You remember those grad students last year from the University who were using dye tracing trying to figure out if that disappearing spring near Cotton Point flowed into the Greystone or the Cave River?"

"Yeah." Ed's interest was piqued. He liked those kids, especially that pretty blonde from St. Louis, and enjoyed hanging around watching them at work.

"You remember that injector unit? It had a long, sharp probe—maybe five or six feet—you could put the nozzle into the ground. It had a big pump and a couple of hoses."

"Yeah, and you'd drop the intake hose into a river or pond. And you could insert the dye capsule into the probe. What about it?" Ed suspected he knew what Mike was thinking and he was thinking he liked the direction this was going.

"Well, Ed, it's kinda like a miniature fracking setup, isn't it?"

"Yeah?" Ed replied with questioning enthusiasm.

"So, we could take a big impact drill, a long bit, and bore a hole next to a post through the hardpan. That's probably only six to eight inches but I gotta 18-inch bit. Little extra never hurt."

"Yeah!" Ed definitely approved.

"Then we could insert the probe into the hole and tap it down with a sledge."

Ed nodded his head, making a mental note he was going to need to find that missing sledgehammer.

"Then we just pump water outta the river into the ground while we pull on the block and tackle haul. The water will push up while we're pulling. Post should pop out of the ground like a cork from a wine bottle."

"Yeah!" Ed agreed wholeheartedly. Then he paused. "Wait a minute, how're we gonna get a hold of a rig like that?"

"The Conservation Department's got one over in Oakmont. They were doing some dye tracing up at Spring Lake. I think I can come up with some research project or other to get them to lend it to me for a weekend."

"Outstanding!"

So that is how Mike, Ed, Ian, and I ended up standing around a 2005 model of a Spectralite High-Pressure Water Injection System, brought in for the "Preliminary Investigation of the Effects of High-Pressure Water Injection on the Removal of Unwanted Agricultural Structures in the Greystone River Basin."

Ian had enough of Ed's and Mike's mutual admiration party and blurted out, "You guys are morons!"

Ed and Mike paused their mutual admiration. They both looked hurt.

"Watcha mean, Ian?" asked Mike.

"Look, idiots," Ian barked. "You're putting a large amount of water pressure underground, right?"

"Yeah?" said Ed, dubiously.

"And that red clay, when it gets wet, is going to act like a seal, like an earthen dam. And that pressure's gonna build and build, till all the sudden, that dam's gonna bust and there'll be hell to pay, not to mention the undertakers to separate your two worthless, fence-post impaled carcasses so that they can bury your sorry asses in separate pine boxes." He followed these observations with several, unexpected, and anatomically specific expletives.

This was pretty strong language for Ian, who generally is an agreeable person. Agreeableness became him, and his current contrarian behavior seemed alien. Not quite like X-Files alien, but pretty strange, nevertheless.

"Ian, there's no call for that," I said. "It may turn out okay, but, if it doesn't, these two idiots will only have themselves to blame."

I turned to look at Ed and Mike while continuing to talk to Ian. "Besides, Spademeyer's Funeral Home could use the business." I chuckled evilly. It was as though I was relishing the thought of Ed and Mike being in self-inflicted pain. Not a lot of pain. Just enough to be retribution for the loss of a full day on the river. Was I really so shallow? Apparently so.

Ed and Mike shook their heads and climbed into Mike's truck pulling a trailer with the Spectralite strapped on board. They drove down the gravel drive, heading out toward Titus's field.

"Guess we should go too," said Ian without enthusiasm.

I nodded in agreement. "Yeah, somebody's gotta let Spademeyer know where to pick up the bodies." An evil chuckle broke out again. This time it was Ian. I shuddered a little. Were evil chuckles contagious? We got into Ian's truck.

A short while later, we pulled into Titus's field and stopped about 100 or so feet away from the rig that Mike and Ed were setting up at a fence post. Ian and I looked at each other. We looked at Mike and Ed. We looked at their block-and-tackle set up. We looked at each other again. We knew what the other was thinking—staying in the truck, with the AC on, and drinking beer was definitely what the situation called for. Ian fished around in a cooler in the club cab and brought out two beers, handing me one. It was cheap stuff, Old Milwaukee, but it was cold, and I was grateful.

Ed yelled at us, "You guys coming over to help us?"

Ian rolled down the window. "Nah," he said, "Someone's got to be outta the way to call Spademeyer's."

"Well, what about you, Alastair?"

"Think I'll stay with Ian. He's got this cheap awful beer that needs drinking, and you just don't let your friends drink cheap awful beer alone." We glanced at each other. Another evil chuckle, in stereo.

"Suit yourself," said Ed. We could tell he was thinking, "Why don't those guys want to have fun with Mike and me?" And Ian and I were thinking, "Oh, we'll have fun, alright, Ed. Just you wait." The evilness of the chuckle which followed that thought could best be described as monstrously sinister. Ian and I were getting pretty good at this. But the gradual mellowing effect of the beers soon took out the evil and replaced it with an occasional companionable guffaw.

Ed turned and busied himself by checking all the chains. He gave the haul a little experimental tug. He looked over at Mike, satisfied everything was a go on his end.

Meanwhile, Mike lugged the supply hose down to the river. He slipped down the steep bank and waded out a bit to make sure the hose would draw well. He clambered back up the bank, sauntered over to the injector rig, and made sure all the hose connections were snug.

Mike joined Ed back at the fence post. He opened a toolbox and fished around for a one-inch diameter drill bit. This was the 18-inch-long bit he mentioned earlier. Finding it, he inserted it into a big impact drill, bent over next to the post, and began to bore through the clay hardpan. Thirty seconds later, Mike stood back up (feeling a twinge in his back and shoulder), blew the clay dust off the bit, and surveyed his work with approval. He set the drill down on the open toolbox and moved over to the injector. He positioned the probe in place, gave it a few taps with the sledge, firmly seating it in the clay. He looked carefully around the setup. Satisfied, he looked over at Ed who gave him a thumbs up. Mike pulled on the starting cord for the pump's gas engine. Surprisingly, for government equipment, it started on the first tug.

"Verrrrr," said the pump.

"That's funny," said Ian, "Never heard a pump go 'verrrr' before." He took a long sip of his beer.

I took a sip of my beer in agreement. "Yep, me neither," I replied.

After a minute or two, I suppose the pressure was really increasing underground. The pump began to say, "Spurrrr."

"I don't like that," I said, firmly. "Pumps should never say 'spurrrr.'"

"No," said Ian. "They should definitely stick to 'verrrr.' Pumps say 'verrrr' very nicely. Bad manners to say 'spurrr.'"

We sipped our beers in mutual agreement. Five more minutes went by.

"Why do you think they haven't started tugging on the haul yet?" I wondered idly.

"Guess they're wanting to really build up the pressure."

The pump then indicated it couldn't decide whether it liked saying "verrrr" or "spurrrr" better, so it began to alternate rapidly between the two to figure out its preference.

"Verrrr-spurrrr, verrrr-spurrrr, verrrr-spurrrr."

"Don't like that at all," I opined.

"Nah, the pump needs to make up its mind. Can't very well go around saying 'verrrr' then 'spurrrr' then 'verrrr-spurrrr.' Ain't natural."

"Yep. Say, Ian, how about another beer?"

Ian dug around and brought out another plus one for himself.

"Cheap beer," said Ian. "Sorry."

"Nah, it's alright," I replied. "Besides, it's cold."

"Yep."

"Verrr-spurrrr, verrrr-spurrrr, verrrr-spurrrr," said the pump, ignoring our conversation.

About then Mike seemed to have concluded there was enough pressure built up. He yelled over to Ed. We couldn't hear him, but figure it had to be something along the lines of "You ready to pull?"

Ed nodded his assent and they both took hold of the haul.

"Verrr-spurrrr, verrrr-spurrrr, verrrr-spurrrr."

I could see Mike mouthing, "One, two . . ."

He never got to "three." About when he should have gotten to three, the pump said, "Verrrr-spurrrr, verr-rr-SPURRRR, SPURRR, SPURR, SPUR, SPOUTAH!"

The ground, evidently thinking that this was a signal, gave its own "SPOUTAH," followed by several "Blurb-blurb-blurbs."

Ian said he didn't care much for the "SPOUTAH."

"Yeah," I said. "'SPOUTAH' was uncalled for."

Then we watched with almost clinical detachment as a six-foot high geyser of red clay-ladened water came erupting from the ground around the post.

"That's probably not good," I observed.

"Yeah," Ian agreed. Obviously, he was becoming his agreeable self again. Kinda nice.

By this time, Mike and Ed dropped the haul and quickly stepped back about 50 feet from the post.

"Hmm," said Ian. "May not have to call Spademeyer's after all."

"Well," I said thoughtfully. "Maybe they should step back a bit more."

As if on cue, Mike and Ed backed up another 50 feet, facing the geyser, until they bumped into the front end of Ian's truck. They both jumped in panic, turned to see it was just us, and returned to staring at the cataclysm.

Then three events happened almost simultaneously. The hose which ran from the pump to the probe blew off its connector, shooting water liberally around the work site. Freed from this impediment, the pump increased its vocabulary, adding, "SHOW-WOW, SHUSH-SHUSH-SHUSH, SHOW-WOW."

"That's new," I observed.

"Yeah," said Ian. "It's really a big day for . . ."

He didn't finish. Something must have finally broken loose underground. The fence post shot out of the ground. It sailed maybe 15 feet straight up, arced toward the fence, and insisted on tangling itself in the fence wire. Now, firmly anchored, but with energy to spare, it began to spin around like a windlass, pulling the fencing loose from three adjacent posts.

"POOP-WANG!" said the fence, adding several more "WANGS" for emphasis.

"That's a new word." Ian remarked.

"Mmm, maybe two," I countered.

Ian nodded. "Could be right."

Meanwhile, Ed and Mike stood frozen, locked to Ian's truck's front end as though they'd been superglued in place.

The post finally stopped its dizzying dance. Looking down along the line of the fence, we saw that the fencing and the post were wrapped around one another in a galvanized cocoon.

"Hmm," said Ian.

"Yeah," I agreed.

"Well, it seems to have stopped spinning around. You reckon it's safe to go turn off the pump?"

"Probably." I replied.

We got out of the truck and sauntered down to the pump, avoiding the gushing water. Sauntering seemed the appropriate means of locomotion. It was like unhurried order in the midst of chaos visited on earth in the form of an Ozark catastrophe. Ian shut down the pump and the water coming out of the river slowed down then stopped altogether.

"SHOW-wow, shush, spurrrr, verrrr, sh-sh-sh-sh." Silence

"I liked the 'sh-sh,' very restful." I noted.

"Yeah, kinda fitting, like it was saying, 'Okay, I'll be quiet now.'"

We turned and headed back to the truck. When we arrived, Mike and Ed began to stir. They looked over the disaster in disbelief.

We nodded at them and then climbed into the truck. Ian started it and put it into reverse.

"Hey, wait a minute!" shouted Mike.

Ian put on the brakes, put the truck in park, and wound down his window. "What?"

"Aren't you guys going to help us with this?" asked Mike, gesturing in the general direction of the red clay-splattered equipment.

"Nah, we just came to drink beer. Oh, and call Spademeyer's if we needed to. Didn't have anything to do with you," said Ian.

I looked up from the now empty cooler. "Yeah, and since all the beer's gone and there's nobody dead, I figure it's time to go."

"You're right, Alastair. Let's go."

He put the truck back in reverse, backed up in an arc for a few feet, then put it in drive. And drive we did, all the way back to Ed's place. We knew Ed never locked up his place, so we went in, raided his fridge, made up some ham sandwiches, grabbed a six pack, and went out on the porch to wait for Ed and Mike to return.

"Wonder what Mike's research report's gonna say?" I asked.

"I don't know," said Ian. "I hope he quotes the pump, though. I thought it had some important things to say."

"Yep," I replied.

About five hours later, Ed and Mike returned. Ed climbed out of Mike's truck and Mike immediately pulled away, the trailer with the injector system bumping along dutifully behind, leaving a trail of red water in its wake.

"Gonna take a shower," said Ed as he saw us on the porch. "Help yourself to the beer and whatever's in the fridge."

"Already have," answered Ian.

"Good ham," I opined.

"Yeah," agreed Ian. I liked agreeable Ian, and I told him so.

"Better than the way you were behaving when I first got here."

"Well, I probably had low blood sugar or something."

"Or something," I agreed, but thought that a few beers were the likely answer for the transition.

The next day I got up early and joined Ed for a breakfast of oatmeal and toast in his jumbled kitchen. We didn't speak of the events of the day before. Instead, Ed asked if I still wanted to go floating the Greystone. I said that I'd rather spend the morning fishing instead. When we finished our breakfast, we loaded our fishing gear into Ed's truck and drove to the river, swinging by his barn first to grab his 10-foot john boat. He drove down to the confluence of the Greystone and the Cave where we put in. It was a good morning fishing. We didn't catch much trout (a couple of small ones), but we did reel in three good-sized bass and about a dozen bream. Ed caught a six-pound channel cat. I let Ed keep the fish.

We returned to Ed's where we unloaded my meat from one of his many freezers and loaded it into the coolers I had in the truck bed. And I got on the road. As I pulled out on to US 60, I started thinking about the day before. "Verrrr." "Spurrrr." I chuckled to myself, though not evilly.

I called Ed the next week to thank him for the meat and his hospitality. I asked about the folks in Derry County, and he filled me in on the gossip.

Finally, though, I had to bring the issue up. "Okay, what happened over at Titus's field? You ever get any of that fence?"

"No, Mike found out he didn't need it," said Ed with disgust.

It transpired that a couple of days after I left, Nora's mom passed away. She was quite old and infirm and was ready to join her late husband and Jesus. Nora was sad, of course, but relieved as well, as this freed up enough time for her to go back to work full-time as a visiting nurse. With that increased income, plus her share of her mom's modest estate, she could completely remodel the kitchen and the master bath. Maybe even the second bath and add a half-bath for company. What she would not have to do is rely on Mike's hairbrained agricultural scheme.

Mike agreed that pork farming was not for him. He was relieved, to be honest. He got the injector unit back to Oakmont, none the worse for wear, and he slapped together a report that didn't have too many fabrications.

"What about Titus's field?" I asked.

"Oh, well, you know," Ed said. "Ol' Titus just had the construction guys bulldoze the fence into a burn pile. Said he'd have them bury whatever was left."

"Well, I reckon an RV park will sit comfortably on a buried pit with old, rusted wire and fence posts," I replied.

"Probably so, probably so," said Ed reflectively. "You never can tell with Titus or any of the MacKays for that matter."

"Yep, that's right," I replied, thinking, but not saying, "Nor can you tell with any mountain mad scientists."

Boiling Bobcats

It was a crisp, sunny Ozark autumn morning. The foliage was at its best: the vivid yellows of the hickories, the deep crimsons of the maples, the riotous mixtures of golds, oranges, and reds from the assortment of oaks. It was going to be a good day.

I was finally going to take that float trip on the Greystone I had hoped for on my last visit which was aborted by Mike's and Ed's playing around with fence posts. With visions of the lifting morning mists on the Greystone, and the trout basking in the sunlight below the riffles, I smiled broadly as I pulled up the drive to Ed's farm. Yep, still in my Prius.

Parking next to his battered farmhouse, I headed up to the backdoor which led straight into his kitchen. I noted, with a little concern, that there was a strange smell wafting toward me, like a combination of soup and spoiled meat. "Think I may skip lunch," I muttered.

I walked through the door and sniffed. I regretted it immediately. Outside, the race between the soup and spoiled meat smells was an undecided contest. Inside, it was clear that the soup was losing the election by the high double digits.

"What in God's name is that smell!?!" I shouted. I don't know why I was shouting. Other than the sound of boiling coming from a battered pot on the stove, the kitchen was pretty quiet.

"Hey, Alastair," greeted Ed. "Come on in."

I reluctantly came in and, with even greater reluctance, closed the door behind me. It was, after all, pretty chilly outside.

"What in God's name is that smell?" I repeated, though in a more conversational, inquiring tone.

"Groan! Urgh! Gahh!"

I turned to look over by the kitchen table. Seated there, wrinkling his nose and coughing, a thousand olfactory miseries written on his face, was Allen. I looked questioningly at him, hoping he could shed some light on the situation. He coughed and gagged loudly, wiping tears and perspiration from his face. It was clear enlightenment wasn't coming from that source any time soon.

I looked around at Ed. He was standing nonchalantly at the stove, stirring at the pot with no more concern than if he was cooking chicken soup. He was *not* cooking chicken soup, or if he was, that bird had been dead since sometime last year. He placed the lid on the pot, which lessened the smell from slaughterhouse- to garbage-can-level, swatted ineffectually at some steam, and grinned broadly at me.

"I'm boiling a bobcat's head," he said, as if that were a normal day in the life of Ed's kitchen.

I am definitely skipping lunch. I backed into the doorway leading into the dining room.

Ozark folks used to make soup (usually with dumplings) out of a lot of different kinds of animals. Other than the usual barnyard critters, anything from squirrels, to rabbits, to possums were fair game for the pot. But bobcat heads? Not when there was Campbell's.

I turned to Allen. "Why are you sitting there? This is awful!"

"Well, it is my bobcat head," said Allen, only further adding to the mystery and misery of the situation.

Getting up from the table and grabbing me by the shoulder, Allen ushered me back outside. Gulping in fresh air and wiping our faces with our handkerchiefs, we slumped in silent suffering against the Prius.

When we recovered, Allen explained the matter. It seems there is a lot of money for well-cleaned, intact animal skulls. The scientific supply houses cannot keep up with the demand and they pay a premium for good specimens. The day before, Allen came across a road-kill bobcat. Coming to a stop on the side of the road, Allen went to investigate the corpse. It was a mangled mess, likely had been there for a few days. But the head was perfectly intact. I wish I could affirm that Allen didn't say "purr-fectly." I can't.

"Purr-fectly! Get it? Get it?"

I refused to respond.

I won't go into the grisly details of how he detached the head from the body. But being a late bobcat, the feline probably didn't care.

Somehow, he talked Ed into boiling the skin and meat and such off the bones. I suspect Allen's reason for asking to use Ed's kitchen was that he was happily married and wanted to stay that way. Ed, however, had gone through a divorce last year (his third) and was now a confirmed bachelor. Who cared what Ed's kitchen smelled like? Ed didn't.

About a half an hour later, Ed came banging out the back door, a steaming pot of boiled bobcat head held firmly by two dishtowel wrapped hands. He smiled as he passed us.

"Smells good, don't it boys! Just like mamma used to make." He snickered at our renewed retching.

Going about 50 feet away from the house, Ed began pouring off the bobcat broth, taking care to hold the lid in place in order not to lose any bones. He set the pot down on the gravel drive to cool and placed a fair-sized, flat rock on the lid.

"To keep the critters out," he noted with a grin.

He came back toward us and tossed the greasy dishtowels onto the back steps leading to the door.

"What's bugging you guys? Surely not that bobcat head!" he said, eyes gleaming mischievously. "I mean, Alastair, you were a marine scientist in the Navy and a high school biology teacher. You had to have dealt with some pretty obnoxious odors."

"True," I replied, "but I was always in a lab with good ventilation or outdoors. And when smells got too bad, there was always a surgical mask and Vicks. Worse come to worse, a good respirator."

"Weenie," Ed replied.

Ordinarily, I would have come back at him with a biting retort, but I couldn't. He was right. Smells were always my Achilles heel. Back when I taught high school, I dreaded the annual two weeks of cat dissections in Anatomy and Physiology. The smell of formalin permeated everything: my clothes, my hair, my beard, my skin, my lunch. Gahh! I kept the ventilator hoods running full blast when the cats were out of their odor-proof polyethylene bags. (Yeah, I know, cats and bags.)

The first week, when the bags were initially opened, the smells were so powerful that I brought a huge shop fan from home. The resulting roar may have added to the hearing damage I incurred in the Navy, but at least my eye and nose watering were reduced from floods to mild torrents. God, I hated those cats. I am a cat person (easier to travel with cats from one Navy base to another). But those cats . . .! And the bobcat head only confirmed my view that the reason for cats was to sit in windows and stare with ineffectual malignity at impudent robins eating worms on the lawn. Not science.

Yeah, weenie.

Chemistry and Chaos

A short, post-bobcat head time later, Allen, Ed, and I were loading two canoes into the back of Ed's truck, along with paddles, life jackets, and coolers of beer and sandwiches. I checked the latter for the presence of suspicious lunch meat. They were good, just some more of Ed's delicious ham from his last hog butchering. We climbed in the truck and headed toward the Greystone.

"Why two canoes, Ed? There's only three of us," I asked.

Allen answered for Ed. "My brother, Josh, is meeting us down by the put-out. He's already parked his truck by the pull-out and got a ride from Mike back to the landing."

Josh was a fun guy and a great fisherman. A fly fisherman, who fished for the simple art of the perfect cast and not, as most Ozarkans, for food. He tied his own flies and would always bring his tying equipment to create whatever insect was hatching at the moment. His casts, with expert double-hauls and rolls, were acts of incredible, heartbreaking beauty. His presentations were as soft as the down feathers he used, the line alighting on the water with no more disturbance than a leaf falling on the river. I was glad he decided to join us.

Josh used to teach high school chemistry, but for reasons he never explained, he left teaching, went to law school, and became an attorney specializing in environmental law at a prestigious firm (Vandervort and Clyde) in St. Louis. He was made a senior partner last fall and was unable to come down to the Greystone as much as he liked. Today was a special treat for him.

We met Josh at the landing, paired up (I got to go with Josh), put the canoes in the river, loaded them up with our gear and supplies, and pushed off into the current. We paddled in amiable silence, enjoying the sunlight playing with the morning mist before whisking it away as the day grew warmer.

About a half mile downstream, we easily shot through a set of class II rapids and entered a long, calm stretch of the river. I paddled slowly in the stern, my well-practiced J-strokes hardly making a ripple. Josh assembled his fly rod and expertly tied a dry fly to the tippet. He stood up carefully in the bow and began to work his magic. I watched him cast with awestruck admiration. The rod moved like a long magic wand, casting spells across the water.

After about 15 to 20 minutes of enchantment, with no fish rising to take his fly, he sat down to tie on a different lure. In the stillness, a question arose in my mind.

"Say, Josh," I began quietly, "why did you quit teaching chemistry and become a lawyer? I mean, other than the money."

He set his rod across the gunwales and sat down, looking off into space, collecting his thoughts.

"Well, I enjoyed teaching, especially when I was at Oakmont. But there came a day, a particular day, mind you, when I knew that it just wasn't for me."

"How's that?"

Josh began a story which to this day is a source of humorous astonishment when I think back on it.

One day, Josh had his AP Chemistry students do an experiment to show how to sublimate naphtha crystals. Working in pairs at the long, black counter-topped lab benches, with a water and gas supply for each station, the students set up beaker stands over Bunsen burners. They placed beakers full of water (called a water bath), and atop the beaker they placed a triangular frame into which they nestled a small ceramic crucible containing the crystals. Each crucible had a matching ceramic lid, which the budding chemists set to one side. As long as the water bath didn't boil dry, the temperature remained a constant 100° C and they could safely change the crystals directly from a solid to a gas. This process is called sublimation. If they failed to follow this simple direction, the naphtha would ignite.

Of course, this in fact happened. One of the pairs of lab partners allowed their beaker to boil dry. As Josh had warned, instead of sublimating, the crystals caught fire.

Now, the proper procedure in such an event is to calmly pick up the crucible lid with tongs and set it on top of the crucible, thereby extinguishing the flame. No harm done. They did not do that. Instead, they grabbed the tongs, picked up the crucible, and dumped the flaming naphtha into the trough which ran down the center of the long lab benches. Well, wrong procedure, but it would have been okay, except . . .

Ah, this was a big "except." Earlier in the day, the first-year chemistry students were experimenting with benzene, a highly flammable chemical. Josh had stepped out of the room to talk to the principal in the hallway outside the lab. Not wanting to bother with the disposal bins which were filled with inert, cat litter-like clay granules, they simply dumped their individually small, but collectively large, amounts of benzene into the trough. Obviously, the mixture of flaming naphtha and benzene wasn't a happy combination.

Wait, it gets worse.

At the beginning of each year, chemistry students spend a full week going over lab procedures, including an entire day on safety. One of the cardinal rules of lab safety is you never put water on a liquid fire. This spreads the fire and water sometimes causes flaming chemicals to explode.

Well, you know what happened. A faucet on the lab bench was turned on and a sheet of flame traversed the entire length of the trough. It all took place in less than three seconds.

Josh started up from his desk and beheld the conflagration. Pretending to have more composure than he actually had, he went to the wall-mounted CO_2 fire extinguisher, quickly covered the distance to the flaming trough, pulled the safety pin, and squeezed the handle. A small poof of gas escaped, then nothing. It seems that Sid Gillespie, the physical science teacher, had recently shown his class that you could freeze cans of Coke with the CO_2 emitted by the extinguisher and had neglected to have it recharged.

Cursing Mr. Gillespie with a stream of expletives his students were pretty sure were not allowed by the teacher's manual, Josh threw the extinguisher across the room, getting a pretty good distance and scattering some lab stools (and some students). He ran over to get the fire blanket.

The fire blanket is made of asbestos (and probably other environmentally unfriendly substances). It was stored on a reel, kind of like the old movie screens, but unlike the screens it was supposed to detach when fully extracted. It did not come loose. It transpired that the facilities crew had used the blanket as a paint drop cloth when they painted the lab last summer and had put it back in its reel with wet paint still on it. This paint adhered the blanket to the reel and when Josh pulled down on it sharply, it came off the wall and crashed into the adjacent reagent cabinet. Large bottles of acids, bases, and other chemicals came crashing down on the floor, shattered, and did what acids and bases do well when mixed. It was not a happy meeting.

Josh stood staring at the catastrophe for a moment, went to the storage closet where he kept some buckets of sand, hurried back to the trough, and poured the contents on the fire, extinguishing the flames.

Meanwhile, a freshman came running into the lab. The school had a habit of using freshmen during their study halls to run messages to the teachers. This freshman, looking for Josh, found he was not in a position to deliver his messages.

Josh didn't know who it was that started yelling at the freshman, but soon the entire class joined in a chorus. "You've been exposed to dangerous chemicals! You gotta get under the shower! Get under the shower!" (Chemistry labs have emergency showers and eye wash stations to wash away chemical contaminants.)

Now, if the freshman was smart, he would have realized he hadn't yet been exposed to anything harmful and could simply step out of the room. If he were really smart, he would have run to the office and reported the disaster. But he wasn't any kind of smart, and so he ran to the shower and pulled down on the metal handle and received a deluge of water flowing at the OSHA-required rate of 60 gallons per minute.

Ordinarily, the drain at the base of the shower would have been able to, more-or-less, handle the water. Sadly, the same crew that painted the walls had also dumped their buckets in which they washed their paint brushes down that same drain, clogging it with cheap latex paint. So, that 60 gallons per minute spread across the floor into the area where the acids and bases had by now neutralized each other into harmless water and salts and from thence into the science faculty office which adjoined the lab. Ben Stuart, the "biology for dummies" teacher, was in the office and came running into the lab—he saw the drenched freshman, the excited, not to say, frantic chemistry students, and a dazed Josh. Mr. Stuart, smarter than the freshman, quickly returned to the faculty office and called administration. The principal, with two or three of the slow-witted facilities crew, came running into the lab to investigate and mop up.

"So, anyhow," said Josh, wrapping up his story. "Sid was reprimanded, the guys who had painted the lab were fired, and the freshman was sent home."

"But it sounds like you didn't do anything wrong. I mean, considering the situation, you saved the day," I replied.

"Yeah, that's eventually how the principal figured it, though he thought maybe somehow I coulda kept control of those idiots who told that stupid freshman to get under the shower. I asked him how exactly was I gonna do that, what with the fire and the acids and such, and he let the matter go."

"So that's why you're no longer teaching chemistry."

"Yep. When the contracts came out for the next year, the principal insisted that I get a substantial pay raise. I looked at the contract, I looked at him, and shaking my head, said, 'There is not enough money in the district's entire budget to convince me to stay.' He said he understood and hoped they could find a replacement even half as good as me. I thought to myself, 'If he's half as good as me, God help the man. Hell, if he was as good as me.'"

Josh stood back up and flicked his line where he thought he saw a swirl in the river. A beautiful rainbow trout rose to the fly, snapped it up, and he expertly set the hook. He retrieved the fish and found it was a nice three-pounder. He set down his rod, stooped down to the river, and released the fish.

"This is a good day," he reflected, standing back up and getting ready for his next cast.

I watched him with awe, taking in his three-part dance with the rod, the line, and the river. I thought to myself, "Yes, it is a good day."

Adele Crockett

I want to be charitable about Granny Adele. I really do. Because she was a fine woman, maybe the finest, but, at least for a long while, not the way most folks measure such things. It'll take a bit of "storying" to explain this, so you might as well sit a spell.

Adele Crockett (as was) was born in Derry County in a cabin along Derry Creek in 1916, one year before her daddy, Furman, went off to the Great War; a year after her sister, June, was born; three years after her sister, Sally, was born; and four years after her mama, May, and her daddy were married. Obviously, May and Furman Crockett were in an all-fired hurry to have a family (or in a hurry to have a son, after two false starts). Later, when she understood the way of things, it was a source of secret embarrassment to Adele. Why in the world did they have to have three children back-to-back-to-back like they did?

Adele wasn't exactly ugly. She just took plain to a whole new level. She was always tall for her age, especially for a woman. She stood maybe five foot eight or nine. But she never stooped, always stood straight, like her daddy, before he went off to the War. She was, I guess you could say, slender, but not in a Hollywood sort of way, more along the lines of a hickory pole. She had no figure to speak of, flat as a board front and back. Her brown hair was exactly the wrong shade of brown (sort of a brown trying to decide if maybe it was really grey), and its frizzy texture could not be tamed by any amount of brushing and hair pins.

Her eyes were small, widely spaced, and of an indeterminate color, neither brown nor green, but some muddy mixture of the two, which was about 15 miles of rutted country road away from being alluring. Yet, I hasten to add, there was a certain spark of intelligence there. Her face was gaunt and hollow, both old and wise before her time, and showed a patient calmness, regardless of what came her way. Her nose, on a man, might be considered distinguished, but on a woman, well, "Bless her heart."

She seldom spoke, but when she did her voice was scratchy and thin, kind of like the creak of an old rocking chair. She never sang on Sundays at the services at Derry Creek Baptist Church. She just sort of mouthed the words quietly to herself. How she wished she could sing. She did love the old hymns. And she loved Jesus, whom she knew wouldn't judge her by her looks (or her voice).

I heard tell that elementary school was a living hell for her—taunted for being too tall, too thin, too squeaky-voiced, and too plain. She left school as soon as she could, which was sixth grade, back in the day. She was sad about that, because she had a good mind, loved to read, and she had a fairly good head for numbers. She especially loved the Bronte sisters and Jane Austen. *Sense and Sensibility* was her favorite, she read it dozens of times. She hoped, in her heart of hearts, that one day she would find an Edward for her Elinor. Someone who looked past her plainness and saw the real her, someone who loved her for her heart and her mind. She would lay down the book, look off into the distance, and sigh. That would never be for me, she thought, not in Derry County, not in a million lifetimes.

As you might guess, intelligence in a woman in Derry County, with no looks or money or land to go with it, was not considered a desirable trait. It got her in trouble in school. The teacher at the little one-room schoolhouse at the backside of Derry Creek loved her dearly. Adele would patiently raise her hand to all the questions. You would think the other students would feel some relief, not having to answer the questions themselves, but no, they resented her. Calling her the teacher's pet was far and away the most pleasant thing they said about her.

After school, when the teacher was inside sweeping up the classroom, the other girls frequently waylaid Adele, throwing her books into an Osage orange thicket and tossing her papers in the air. Adele would calmly gather up her school things, straighten her homemade dress, push back the frizzy brown hair (how she hated that hair) from her mud-colored eyes, and trudge back to her home.

Adele's home was on the east side of Derry Creek, the "unfashionable neighborhood" of the Creek, if it could be said there was a fashionable neighborhood anywhere in that part of Derry County. The house was built in the 1860s. It was an old, three-room dog-trot cabin with square-hewn logs, the chinking carefully whitewashed. There was a sleeping loft above a parlor (as folks used to call it) on one side, and a kitchen and a small bedroom on the other. The cabin may have been old, but it was neat and clean. Her mama kept a firm hand over the household. The rug in the parlor may have been a bit threadbare, but it was regularly taken out, thrown over the clothesline, and beaten to shake out the dirt and bits of straw that are naturally tracked into a farmhouse. The quilts on all the beds were patchwork (back before they became fashionable), but they were skillfully sewn. I'm sure that today May's quilts would fetch hundreds of dollars.

The yard was kept weed-free, the clotheslines were taut, and the path from the road to the house was regularly raked. The large garden, more than an acre, was well tended and bountiful. Its rich limestone soil produced sweet corn; big, ruby-rich tomatoes (the kind they call "heirloom" today); pole beans by the bushel; crisp, sweet, yellow onions; radishes; lettuce; an assortment of greens (mostly collards); cabbage (for sauerkraut); and so much more. There were two apple trees in front of the cabin whose fruit was juicy and slightly tart, perfect for eating or baking.

The well-maintained chicken pen, with its whitewashed coop, was populated by a motley mix of hens of indeterminant breed, ruled over by an old black rooster who ensured his harem minded their p's and q's (or so they let him think). From this flock came many a delicious egg, the yolks a deep yellow, almost orange. There would be an occasional old biddy that would end up in the stewing pot and, maybe once a month, the odd fryer for Sunday dinner.

Out beyond the chickens was a spring house—a sort of stone shelter built into the side of the hill where cold, limestone-sweetened water would bubble out, making a space nearly as cold as a refrigerator where you would store milk, cream, butter, fresh fruit, maybe even homemade cheese (kinda like ricotta). Just downhill from the spring house was a shallow pool, built for cooling watermelons and sweet tea. My wife, Elsbeth, and I once visited the old Crockett place. The spring house and the pool were still there, as well as the stone foundations of the cabin, but the cabin itself was long gone.

The Crocketts used to have a sow and a milk cow, but when Adele's daddy came back from the War missing an arm and about half his senses, May decided to sell the cow and the pig. Given how much attention Furman needed, it was too much work for her. Adele was just a baby then and didn't remember them, but her mama did, and she missed them. So, May would sell some of her produce, a quilt or two, some canned tomatoes, and take in washing to buy bacon, fat back, milk, cornmeal, flour, and such, for Adele and her two older sisters. With her hard work, and Furman's pension, they made out relatively well.

Unlike for some poor folks in the Ozarks, food wasn't a worry for the Crocketts. True, some who lived in Providence might consider it rather plain fare, but Adele's mama could work magic on the woodstove, turning simple ingredients into a mouth-watering feast: crispy-edged corn bread, baked in a cast iron skillet greased with bacon fat (as it should be); pinto beans, flavored with fat back; green beans, cooked with bits of bacon and chopped onions; sliced firm tomatoes, with just a dash of salt and pepper; mixed greens cooked in chicken stock, with just the slightest hint of vinegar to take out the bitterness; golden fried chicken (when they could have it); and May's crowning glory: her chicken and dumplings. The dumplings were lighter than air, the stock was rich with a glistening film of chicken fat dancing across the top of it, and the morsels of chicken would practically melt in your mouth. I know this for a certainty because Elsbeth got May's recipe through Adele (and maybe even some of May's spirit as well, because Elsbeth's chicken and dumplings are a modern-day legend).

Adele got her plain looks from May's mama, while May got her looks from her daddy, a Swede who mysteriously arrived in Derry County to work for the Ozark and Ouachita Timber Company. May was once a pretty woman, blonde haired, blue eyed, and fair complected. But hard work and worry over Furman wore her down to where she looked all over like thin skin stretched over knuckles. But May's eyes were still beautiful and kindly, even when that look of deep concern came over her about her husband's health.

She had every reason to be concerned. Furman was a strong, strapping, though somewhat rawboned, man before he went off to France in 1917. He fought bravely, rose to the rank of sergeant, and won the Star Citation (what is today called the Silver Star) at the Battle of Belleau Wood. But during the Meuse-Argonne offensive, a German shell fell into his trench, taking off his right arm at the elbow, and throwing him up through the air, swirling like a bloody pinwheel. As he flew, he saw the shattered remains of several of the soldiers in his section, men who were his friends, even a couple from Derry County. His body came back down, slamming hard against the mud, but his mind never fully returned to earth. He went back to Derry County a shattered man: shattered body, shattered mind.

Many a young man from Providence or Derry Creek went off to the War with him and he was the section leader for several of them, one of whom was Cletus MacKay. To the people of Derry County, Furman was a hero—truth be told, still so to this day. If, during one of the few times Furman came into Providence, some young insolent pup made fun of him, he would have his ear boxed by the closest man and, upon reaching home, would have his backside tanned by his pa for good measure. For all their "backward ways," most folks in Derry County knew the true worth of a man, and Sergeant Furman Crockett was worth his weight in silver dollars.

It was partly because of Cletus MacKay's (my great grandfather) influence that May found she always got top dollar for her produce, canned goods, and quilts. Of course, the quality was always the best, but still . . . And yet, it wasn't charity, more of an ongoing payment on the debt so many families owed to Furman. For all that everyone acted like this was a secret, May knew, and she accepted it for the sake of Furman and the girls.

As I said earlier, Adele was the youngest of the three Crockett girls, the others being Sally (the oldest) and June (the prettiest). June took after her mama in her looks and by many accounts she was the best-looking girl in all of Derry County. Perhaps it was a good thing June was so beautiful as there was not much to her by way of hard work and even less by way of smarts. But she always counted on some young, handsome, rich man finding her, maybe, when she was in Providence, and he'd carry her away, as far away from Derry County as could be. And she got her wish, as well.

In town during Spring Break, a young University of Missouri student named Willem Vandervort saw her sitting on the bench in front of the Mercantile. Willem was a good-looking young man and one of the descendants of a small group of middle-class Dutch families that settled in the area in the 1870s. (Not that it bears directly on the story, but I went to school with a James Vandervort, who was a cousin, some which way or the other, of Willem. His dad was an optometrist in Oakmont.) June was stunning: a body curvy in all the right places, demanding to be held; blonde hair like sunshine on golden wheat, ordering young admiring swains to run their fingers through it; sapphire blue eyes, commanding adoration from all; a generous smile highlighted by dazzling white teeth and outlined by red lips so luscious it should be against the law not to kiss them; and just the slightest hint of a tan, enough to show her to be healthy, but not so much as to suggest she'd do anything as vulgar as work under the sun.

It only took one look for Willem to become hopelessly enslaved to June.

> Right then and there,
> on the courthouse square,
> where no other boy would dare . . .

he got down on his knees and proposed to her. Didn't even know her, except as what folks said about her. But he didn't care. He had to possess her. For all its initial superficiality, June and Willem proved to be a good match. Willem went back to the University and graduated with a law degree. The ink had barely dried on his diploma before he was offered a job at a prestigious law firm in St. Louis, which he accepted. He immediately returned to Derry County, eloped with June to Oakmont, and got married at the Rhett County courthouse. They were married for 62 years (they both died in 1995), with three sons and a passel of grandchildren, great grandchildren, and great great grandchildren. Willem became a senior partner at the firm. And June? Well, her figure got a lot fuller, but she was very beautiful and very happy till she passed away at 80 years of age just shortly after Willem's death.

Sally was the more religiously inclined of the girls. Not that she had more faith or loved Jesus more than Adele or her mama. It's just that she felt deep in her heart she had to make a show of her faith, and she was determined to become a missionary. Sally was intelligent (though not so much as Adele), good looking (though not so much as June), and hardworking (though not so much as her mama). Since she completed her education at the new Derry County High School (a significant educational accomplishment for a young woman back in those days), and out of no little respect for her daddy, the Derry County Baptist Association sent her to interview with the Southern Baptist Mission Board. They were so impressed with her fervor and intelligence they sent her to LaGrange College (now Hannibal LaGrange College) to prepare her to be a teacher.

Sally was considered a model student by her professors. Over the course of the two-year teacher education program, she got the highest marks ever seen to that date, and yet

she still found time to visit her family in Derry County as
often as she could. That meant she'd have to take the train
from LaGrange, Missouri, to St. Louis, then on to Oakmont.
Once she arrived at the small Frisco Line station, Cletus
MacKay made sure that someone would be there to pick her
up and take her home to Derry County.

After teaching at a school for Black children in Hannibal
for a few years to gain some much-needed experience, Sally
was sent to China in 1935 to be mentored by the Baptist missionary Sophie Stephens Lanneau, a renowned educator and
the principal of the Wei Ling School in Soochow. The original plan was for Sally to learn Mandarin and get experience
in teaching Chinese children, as well as in school administration, before moving on to another school the Mission Board
planned to start in Lu'an. The invasion of China in 1937 by
Japan quickly put an end to that idea. Sally remained with
Miss Lanneau, going with her to Shanghai in 1938 where
she taught at the joint mission school until the school was
closed in 1941. The Japanese forced all American missionaries remaining in China into internment camps in 1943.

Adele was enormously proud of her sister and eagerly
awaited her next letter from China, which continued coming
even after Sally was interned. Each page would be filled with
exotic Chinese writing (she learned her name was spelled 阿
黛尔 and was pronounced a-dai-er). There would be a little
line drawing of an aged Chinese woman selling strange
looking vegetables ("I'll bet you've never seen anything like
that in mama's garden!"). Maybe a slip of rice paper with a
Scripture verse in Chinese. And story after story of unimag-
inable darkness into which the light of the Gospel and good
education must shine: cholera ("Lord, why don't they boil
the water before they drink it?"), malnutrition ("All these
poor people have to eat is rice, not a bit of protein."), abuse
of women ("I saw a man beat his wife to death today in the
fields outside of Soochow and no one said a thing."), pros-
titution (a concept Adele found hard to understand, they

sell their bodies?), and opium ("It's even more deadly than moonshine," a fact Adele found hard to believe).

One day in 1943, the letters stopped. It was hard to get letters to Derry County from Japanese-occupied China, but the Red Cross was normally able to make that happen. Adele hoped it was just that the war made it take longer than usual to arrive. "Maybe they have to go through Switzerland or Spain or some other neutral country." Then one day a letter arrived from Miss Lanneau, just before Christmas 1943. Sally had died at the camp in Shanghai of typhus, just three months before Miss Lanneau and other American missionaries were released in a prisoner exchange. Miss Lanneau went to great lengths in praising Sally for her hard work and her love of the Chinese people and, above all, for her devotion to Jesus. While the letter brought closure, it didn't bring any comfort. For a long time, Adele felt empty, hollow, like an old, lightening-struck oak tree. The tree may look good on the outside, but on the inside, there were nothing but scorch marks.

At the time of Sally's death, Adele had been on her own for some while. June got married and moved with Willem to St. Louis in 1933. A year later, her mama died from pancreatic cancer, a horrible, excruciating disease. In the good Lord's providence, she died quite soon after her diagnosis. Sally left for China a year after that. Daddy died in 1937, though what was left of his mind finally broke with May's death. He really wasn't much more than an empty shell. Adele found him, when he died, lying in bed, white and staring at the ceiling in the small bedroom where he and mama once lay. Maybe, just maybe, there was just a hint of a smile on his lips? Maybe he saw mama? Maybe his mind came back to him enough to know that he really had no one to be heroic for and he could let go of this world. Adele wasn't sure.

She knew she should feel some peace, some release, with her daddy's death. But for some reason it hit her harder than her mama's. She had known, with her mama's death, she would have to look after daddy. June was in St. Louis, Sally was far away in China; it fell to her to run the Crockett household. And that gave her purpose, some measure of happiness even. She could do something, and do it well, that no one else could do. But with her daddy's death, she was the last Crockett living in Derry County, and she had no one "to do for" except herself.

When her daddy died, Adele sold the farm to my great grandpa Cletus MacKay for a price far more than it was worth, at his insistence, and bought a small house on the outskirts of Providence on the Oakmont Road. For some reason or other, the Veteran's Bureau kept sending her daddy's pension to her. She went to the Derry County courthouse to ask about this. She explained that she wasn't a war widow. But they told her to just let it be. So, she did. When the Bureau finally found out, in 1940, the checks simply stopped without explanation. Cletus MacKay used his considerable influence to get her a job in the office of the County Collector (she was quite smart, after all), and there she worked quietly and efficiently for many a year.

Adele had the respect of the citizens of Derry County. Not just because of her daddy (though there was that), but also because she worked hard and kept the collector's office on the straight-and-narrow. No tax receipts were lost under her watch, the tax notices were sent out on time, and she made sure no funds somehow vanished off the books, as was common in the day. The county collector was an elected official, a politician, who was voted in because he was popular, not because he was competent with the tax books. But Adele was competent, to the disappointment of many a sly collector looking to rake off some of the county's revenues. No collector, or any other county politician, would dare cross the daughter of Furman Crockett.

Adele had worked for 25 years at the collector's office when tragedy struck her benefactor, Cletus MacKay. Cletus's wife of 43 years, my great grandma Olivia Jones (as was), died just shy of her 60th birthday. Stroke, just all of the sudden. It was a shock to all, especially Cletus. He had married her young (she was just 17) right after he got back from the War. Theirs was a surprisingly happy marriage, for all that she was a teetotaling, hellfire and brimstone, Landmark Baptist, and he was the premier moonshine distiller in Derry County. Oh, she'd shout at him and cry out to the Lord to save him. But she did love him.

Maybe she was wound a little too tight. Maybe that's why she had the stroke. Maybe. But now she was dead, and Cletus was left heartbroken at the age of 63. He was still a strong, healthy man, wealthy by Derry County standards. And though his children, Josie and Mack, were all grown, he had that big farm to run and timber stands to manage.

Naturally, every widow woman in the county started making eyes at him. No sooner had Olivia been laid to rest in the MacKay family cemetery, than they started bringing by pies and fried chicken and hints that maybe he'd like to come over for dinner next Sunday. Now, understand, folks in Derry County always bring by food for a grieving family, maybe for a week or so after the burial. But these ladies persisted long afterwards, all hoping to catch a rich widower's attention. The way to a man's heart is, after all, through his stomach. This went on for some months until they finally cottoned on that Cletus was not in the market for a new wife.

One day, while preparing a simple bachelor's meal, he got a hankering for chicken and dumplings. He thought back to the last time he had a good pot of that Ozark delicacy. It was not long after Olivia's death, he recalled. Who was it that made them? Then he remembered: it was Adele Crockett. Obviously, Adele's cooking took after her mama's. As soon as this realization struck, he determined right then and there he was going to marry Adele Crockett. Oh, sure she wasn't much to look at, but he reflected that when a man reaches a certain age, he was more interested in comfortable companionship and anyone who could make chicken and dumplings like that was bound to be a comfortable companion.

So, to everyone's surprise, Cletus MacKay, who could have his pick of any pretty widow, set his mind to courting Adele. He began showing up at the collector's office for some piddling, manufactured excuse. Was she sure that she had sent out the tax notices? Did she get his last payment? Was it entered into the books? This exasperated Adele to no end. What was the matter with that man? She knew he knew she was good at her job, the best assistant the courthouse ever saw. He knew he always got his notices. He always got the receipt, written in her own careful neat hand, the very day he came to the office to pay his taxes. Finally, after a word in the collector's ear from Cletus, that worthy official said, "Adele, honey, Ah think ole Cletus is tryin' to spark with you."

Well, she was astonished. Why would Cletus, a man of considerable means, want to marry her, she being as plain as a pole barn? But when Cletus came into the office the next time, Adele made sure to be very nice to him, waving off his pretended concerns with a warmed-hearted, good-natured kindliness. Soon, Cletus was stopping in the office just to spend the time of day. When it was Adele's lunchtime, she accepted Cletus's offer to take her to lunch. Sometimes he'd take her to the Riverside Café, sometimes he'd buy sandwiches and Cokes from the Mercantile and they'd have a picnic right in the courthouse square. She laughed at his stories in her creaky, squeaky way. She expressed genuine concern over the troubles his grandsons Ralph and Titus would get into. And although she wouldn't even touch corn liquor, she murmured appreciatively over Cletus's bragging about his latest batch of the "good stuff." Finally, after almost two years of courting, Adele said, "Cletus MacKay, if you want to marry me, why don't you just say so."

Cletus blinked, he hiccupped in surprise, took in a deep breath, and said, "Adele Crockett, you're one of the finest women Ah know. And Ah'd be right proud iff'n you'd give me your hand in marriage."

Adele looked Cletus over. A fine, tall, handsome man, tanned and strong bodied from hard work. Showing his age, yes, with a white shock of hair and lines running over his face. But they were good-humored lines, laid down as much from laughing as from age, and he had a full head of glorious hair, for all that it was white. And his blue eyes sparkled with intelligence and, yes, love. Love for Adele. Had she finally met her Edward?

Cletus and Adele were married in May of 1965 at the courthouse. In fact, in the courtroom itself, not the county clerk's office. Judge Arnold Williams himself presided. The courtroom was full to the point of bursting, with every notable from Derry County present: the sheriff, the collector, the clerk, the assessor, the prosecuting attorney, the county commissioners, even the local state representative, and all their staffs were present. Even June and Willem came from St. Louis for the affair. Out in the courthouse square, most of Providence seemed to be there, waiting to catch a glimpse of the newlyweds.

Of course, there were a number of Cletus's would-be courters, all those widows standing around mournfully lamenting their lot and passing ugly remarks.

"Just goes to show you, there's no fool like an old fool."

"Why in the world, as rich as he is, would he marry someone like Adele Crockett?"

"Well, you know me, I don't want to say a mean word, but Adele, bless her heart, has always been on the backside of plain."

"He only married her 'cause he felt sorry for her."

"And she's 20 years younger than him."

There was a lot of pondering, as well. "Reckon his kids, Mack and Josie, are okay with their daddy marryin' her? I mean, what's goin' to happen when Cletus dies? Is she goin' to get all that money and property?"

The fact of the matter was Mack and Josie were two of the happiest people at the wedding, except, of course, Cletus and Adele. Further, other than those fussy, mean-spirited widows, *everyone* was happy for Cletus and Adele. They were taken aback, of course, when they heard about the upcoming marriage. But they reflected that, somehow, it seemed only fitting that the daughter of Sergeant Furman Crockett should marry the former Private First-Class Cletus MacKay, for all that she was as plain as homemade lye soap.

Mack and Josie weren't worried about Adele getting all of their father's inheritance. Mack was a prosperous, landed man in his own right and Josie was well-married to Charles Williams, a store owner and butcher in Providence. As their daddy explained to them, before the wedding, he and Adele were agreed: Mack would get the land (and the moonshine business, of course), Josie would get his investments (about a quarter of a million dollars), and Adele would get his bank accounts (around $50,000, all told, in checking and savings), his life insurance (another $50,000), and live in the big house on the farm till she passed away. Adele would sell her house in town, and naturally she'd keep the proceeds from that. Cletus warned them, rather sternly, "Don't you go lettin' on about this. This is family business only." Even after Cletus passed away, nobody else knew about these arrangements except the family lawyer.

Cletus and Adele lived happily together on the MacKay farm. Theirs was a steady, warm love, like the soft glowing coals of an oak fire in a wood stove. Cletus went ahead and handed over the whiskey distilling to Mack (the business was slowing down, in any event) but continued to work as hard as ever on the farm and in managing his timber land. Adele was, to his mind, the perfect wife for a man in his later years. Like her mama before her, she kept a clean house, tended a well-cared for garden, canned the produce, sewed quilts for her now extended family, and set many a delightful table around which the family would gather every Sunday after she got back from church. Her recently gained step-children, grandchildren (even Ralph and Titus), and great grandchildren (of whom I was one of many) dearly loved her and she returned that affection gladly. It was as though all the capacity for love, born in that little dogtrot cabin on the eastside of Derry Creek, was stored up in the years after her daddy died, and now it came out in wave after wave of kindly, motherly affection. It was a source of some small sadness to Adele that mama, daddy, and Sally couldn't have been there for the wedding and see her now, surrounded by the children, grandchildren, and great grandchildren that love and the good Lord's kindness gave her, gifts not of nature, true, but gifts of love, nevertheless.

People would often remark, "She's jist like her mama. 'Course, not in looks, bless her heart, but she has done her mama and daddy proud." Mack and Josie would sometimes quietly say to each other that, while they missed their mama, Olivia, Adele was a darn sight easier to get along with and a true pleasure to be around.

Adele and Cletus had been married for just over five years when Cletus's years of hard work finally caught up with him. He had been out in his timber stand in north Derry County, near the line with Bean County, when he got caught in a sudden storm. He came home soaked through and chilled. The chill soon turned into a fever, followed directly by wracking coughs. At first, he wouldn't see Dr. Updike, the family doctor in Providence, but when the coughs began bringing up blood, Adele put her foot down. She called the doctor, who came right away to the MacKay house. She stood worrying over the bed, wringing her hands somewhat, but mostly composed, while the doctor listened to Cletus's heart and lungs, took his temperature, and observed how grey his face and blue his lips had become. Dr. Updike took Adele into the kitchen, sat down at the well-polished old-fashioned farm table, and stared reflectively at the cup of coffee she set down in front of him. After a few moments, he said, "Adele, it looks really bad. Cletus has pneumonia, a very serious case. We need to take him to the Veteran's Hospital over in Oakmont right away. It'll take too long to get an ambulance here. Can Mack take him?"

Adele nodded quietly and called Mack. "Mack, it's your daddy. He's got the pneumonia and we need to take him to Oakmont, to the VA hospital, right away." She thanked the doctor and the two of them went and sat quietly next to Cletus. She softly said, "Cletus, honey, we need to take you to the Vet'ran's hospital."

Cletus looked bleary eyed, first at the doctor, then at Adele. For a moment, the coughing stopped. He motioned to Adele to come near. He wanted to tell her something. She bent over him, the man she loved so dearly, the man who came and rescued her from her years of lonely sorrow. He gripped her hand with surprising strength, looked at her with passion, concern, and sadness, and drew her close. He whispered something quietly in her ear, then, releasing her hand, he closed his eyes, and quietly passed away. And Adele, well, all her calm patience vanished from her face, and she broke down and wept like a little girl. All the heartache, all the sorrow, all the pain she had kept hidden in her heart for years burst out in high, keening sobs. Her Cletus, her Edward, was gone.

I was a kid living in Germany at the time (1971), my dad being in the Army, so I wasn't there, but as I heard tell in later years, it was a large crowd that gathered in the MacKay cemetery for Cletus's funeral. He didn't want a fuss, and certainly not a church service. Just a simple family gathering around the graveside. That didn't stop half the county from showing up and nigh on to half of them came to the house for the reception. Folks brought sympathetic words and quiet, sorrowful murmurings.

"So sorry about your loss, Adele."

"Cletus was a fine man, Ah know yer gonna miss him, Adele. Heck, we're all gonna miss him."

"It was a lovely service up at the cemetery, Adele, so simple and movin'."

They brought food, of course, but while standing quietly together on the back porch by the kitchen door, Mack and Josie observed that none of it came within a mile of Adele's.

After what they thought was a decent interval, widowers from all over Derry County, and some from Bean County as well, would come to the house, trying to court Adele, being a passable rich widow and all, as they supposed. They'd offer some pretense, like

"Adele, do yah have any wood yah need cuttin'?"

"How about yer roof, does it need lookin' to?"

"What about your garden, does it need tillin'?"

It was ridiculous, of course. Mack took care of all of that. Sometimes he'd kick his sons Ralph and Titus in the rear (metaphorically speaking, sorta) to help out. And they would lend a hand without much grumbling, to the incredulity of those who knew those two ne'er-do-wells. Mack's careful attention for his stepmother was all kindly affection. He was grateful for Adele's love and companionship for his daddy in his last years. Josie, Charles, and their children would come by weekly over from Oakmont to visit and see to any needs Mack hadn't gotten to yet. Adele was happy. Sad, yes, longing for Cletus. But she remembered the five, wonderful years they had together, and she was happy. She prayed every day, thanking Jesus for his goodness and asking that the Lord would look the other way when it came to the sin of making 'shine.

Adele lived a life of quiet peace and gratitude for another 42 years, surrounded by grandchildren, great grandchildren, and even great great grandchildren. She outlived her stepson Mack, who died in 2004, and her stepdaughter, Josie, who died in 2010. Adele passed away in her sleep, with the full assurance of her God's love and grace, at the age of 97 in 2013. Just before she fell asleep for that last time, as she lay in the same bed where Cletus passed away, she reflected on what he said to her just before he passed. With a sudden impulse, she leaned over to the bedside table, took a pencil from the drawer, and picked up the Bible which she read every night before she went to bed. With a firm hand which belied her years, she wrote a short note in the back, set down the Bible and pencil, turned off the light, and closed her eyes, making one last little sigh of happiness and satisfaction.

Elsbeth and I attended Granny Adele's funeral at Derry Creek Baptist Church. The little country church had never been so full. All the extended MacKay family came, along with many a visitor from Derry, Bean, and Rhett Counties. Such was the crowd that some had to stand outside the church, its doors being left open so that they too could join in the old hymns that Adele loved so well. The preacher got choked up when he reminisced about Adele's love for her family and her devotion to the Lord. And so many people wanted to eulogize Adele that he had to cut them off or the funeral would never get finished.

A year later, while at the annual family reunion at the MacKay cemetery, Ralph, Mack's oldest son, came up to me.

"Say, Alastair, what with you bein' a perfessor and all, you should write our family history."

"Actually, I was thinking of doing just that."

"Well, come over after we're finished here, and Ah'll give you the family Bible. It's got all the names, births, and deaths and such."

I said it would be an honor. After we cleared away the tables, folding chairs, and the remains of the meal, saying our goodbyes to family we wouldn't likely see till next year, and making sure my mom had a ride with my cousins back to Oakmont, Elsbeth and I drove over to what had been Mack's place, now being Ralph's. I was surprised, given Ralph's reputation as being more than a little idle, that the house was in good repair, and the garden and yard were well tended. Maybe some of his daddy's and granddaddy's character finally took hold.

We sat down at the table and drank some sweet tea Ralph's wife, Mable, offered us. After some small talk about Derry County and Providence and Cletus and Adele, Ralph excused himself and a few minutes later came back with two books. One was an enormous, leather-bound, well-worn family Bible. In the front, as he promised, was a long list of names, complete with dates of births, marriages, deaths, and scribbled notes as to who was related to whom and even how some of them died.

The other was a much smaller Bible, likewise bound in leather and, if possible, even more well-worn than the first. "This is Granny Adele's Bible. It's got some stuff in it about the Crocketts. Thought you'd like that as well."

I thanked Ralph and Mabel and, excusing ourselves as we had a long drive to make to Little Rock, we got in the car and headed to Oakmont to catch US 67 to drive the three-hour trip back home. Elsbeth soon fell asleep, it'd been a long day, but not before asking, "You okay to drive back? We could stay the night in Oakmont at your mom's."

"No, I'll be okay. I'll listen to a book on a MP3 I bought."

I really didn't pay much attention to the book. Mostly I thought about family and how, living over 200 miles away, I really do miss them. I cherish our annual gatherings, and I chuckled to myself about such colorful characters as Ralph and Titus, even my stern Baptist Aunt Dorothy, who still has no idea that there really is moonshine in the chocolate soak cake.

We got back to our home in Little Rock a little after nine o'clock, Elsbeth waking up as we pulled into the driveway. As we walked through the door, each carrying a suitcase, we were greeted by the friendly smells and sights of home and two querulous cats who complained, "We thought for sure you had abandoned us."

Elsbeth said, sleepily, "I'm still tired, I think I'll head up to bed. You coming?"

"No, I think I'll sit up a bit and look through those Bibles." Murmuring good night, she slipped up the stairs to our bedroom. After setting the suitcases near the steps to be dealt with in the morning, I yawned and stretched, poured myself a glass of bourbon, turned on the light next to my favorite chair, and sat down to read. The cats having followed Elsbeth upstairs, I had the room to myself.

For some reason, I was drawn to Adele's King James Bible. The family Bible could wait for a more thorough examination tomorrow. I thumbed through the book, noting it's carefully underline verses and Adele's clear notes written in the margins.

John 3:16, "For God so loved the world, that he gave his only begotten Son, that whosoever believeth in him should not perish, but have everlasting life."

Ephesians 2:8, "For by grace are ye saved through faith; and that not of yourselves: it is the gift of God."

Roman 3:23-25 "For all have sinned and come short of the glory of God; Being justified freely by his grace through the redemption that is in Christ Jesus: Whom God hath set forth to be a propitiation through faith in his blood, to declare his righteousness for the remission of sins that are past, through the forbearance of God . . ." Standard evangelical Scriptural fare.

But then, flipping back into the Old Testament, a revelation: Song of Solomon 6:3-4, "I am my beloved's, and my beloved is mine: he feedeth among the lilies. Thou art beautiful, O my love, as Tirzah, comely as Jerusalem, terrible as an army with banners."

I chuckled quietly. Granny Adele, you are full of surprises. I continued to browse idly through the Bible, coming at last to the back. Here were more notes, written in that same careful hand. As I came to the last entry, I did a double take. I read it over carefully again, realizing that Adele had written the words right before she died. I confess I teared up and felt a lump in my throat.

I started this story by saying I needed to be charitable about Granny Adele, what with her being so plain and all. What with her hard life, her loneliness, the sad tale of her parents and her sister, Sally. But now that I reflect on it, I don't need to be "charitable" about Granny Adele at all. She lived a long life surrounded by family and love. And, as she wrote in her Bible, the most important love of her life, Cletus, the most important man along Derry Creek, with his dying breath had whispered in her ear, "Adele, honey, you are the most beautiful woman in all the world."

Gimme that Ol' Time Religion

I t was about 9:00 in the morning on a Saturday when I walked into the Riverside Café, the bell on the door tingling a merry little melody. Elsbeth and I were in Providence to fish and canoe the Greystone, but I was taking a break from camping to get some of the Riverside's famous pancakes. Elsbeth was going antique shopping (that is, flea market browsing) and was also going by the Super Save to pick up some more eggs and coffee.

I said "hi" to Edna Simmons, the owner, who was manning the cash register at the front counter.

"Mornin', Alastair," she said. "'Fraid yer crazy friends ain't here today."

"That's okay, Edna. I'm here to have breakfast with Pastor Snider."

"Oh, okay. He's in the back room."

(Edna was the wife of Bat Simmons, the owner of the Mercantile across the street on the courthouse square.)

"Thanks, Edna."

I went to the back room, a largish dining area that the Kiwanis and the Lions Clubs use for their meetings. I saw Pastor Snider sitting in the corner with some of the other local pastors who, he told me, met regularly for fellowship.

Tom Snider was the pastor of a Lutheran congregation (Zion Lutheran) in Providence, established about 100 years ago to serve the small but influential German community in Derry County. Like the German population, Zion was a small church, only about 20-30 people showing up on a Sunday. An older minister (74), Pastor Tom eagerly took the call to Providence after serving as the senior pastor at a large congregation in St. Louis for some 20 years. For many years, Tom and his wife, Martie, came to Derry County to float the rivers and fish, and Zion was his idea of what retirement should look like. He got to regularly preach and celebrate the Eucharist. Otherwise, it was an undemanding assignment and it allowed for plenty of time to enjoy his remaining years. Elsbeth and I would worship at Zion when we were in Providence, and we considered it our spiritual home away from home.

"Morning, Pastor Tom," I said.

"Morning, Alastair," he greeted. "Let me introduce you to my pastor friends."

He gestured around the table. "This is Brother John Hopkins, pastor of First Baptist over on Main Street. And this is Reverend Tim Nelson, pastor at First Methodist, which is just down the street from Brother John. And this is Father Neil McCready, who's the pastor of St. Michael's and, also, Holy Family in Wilmot.

I greeted these men of God and joined them at the table. Edna came in and poured me some coffee.

"Whatcha have, Alastair?"

"Pancakes, two eggs over medium, and bacon."

"Like always, huh?"

"Yep."

When Edna left, I looked around the table. Brother Hopkins I knew by reputation. He's been the pastor at First Baptist for years. (Like most towns in the Ozarks, the Baptists are far and away in the majority, the Methodists being a distant second.)

However, the other two I didn't know, which wasn't surprising, given their denominations' practice of reassigning ministers every five years or so. They were both young men (at least to me, maybe in their early 30s) and seemed very much at home with their fellow clergy. This was pretty unusual in a small Ozark town like Providence where religion was a favorite topic for debate. But, I figured, all four were educated men and likely a bit more ecumenical in their outlook.

"So, anyhow, this is Dr. Alastair Spring," continued Pastor Snider. "He's the Dean of the College of Education down in Little Rock. His mom's family's from around here, and he and his wife, Elsbeth, worship at Zion when they're in town."

"Spring, eh," said Brother Hopkins. "Don't recall a Spring family from around here."

"No, sir. But my mom's family are the MacKays and the Joneses from over along Derry Creek."

"Oh, of course," he said. "Got some of them attending at First Baptist, now. I heard they were fed up with the tininess of Derry Creek Baptist and wanted to come some place with a youth ministry. So, they came to us."

"I wish we even had some youth at St. Michael's," replied Father McCready, wistfully. "All I've got is about four or five families. But they're pretty faithful, so there's that. We do get a few devout folks during summer vacation but, of course, after a week or two they're gone."

Father McCready's two small churches formed a single parish which served the last remnants of the old Irish population which settled in Derry County in the mid-1800s to work the timber. They were nearly wiped out during the Civil War, seeing how nearly everyone, regardless of wartime sympathies, had a passionate antipathy toward them. Those who managed to survive created a tightknit community which preserved much of their identity for two or three generations. But, with the movement westward of the timber companies and the lack of job opportunities, most of their young people headed to St. Louis and have been doing so for some time. The only ones who remained were those who managed to carve out some farms (mostly dairy) from the rocky plateaus in western Derry and eastern Adair counties. Through hard work and no little perseverance, they became prosperous folks, but, other than their religion, they were thoroughly enculturated with the rest of the Derry County population.

"It's tough," agreed Reverend Nelson. "Tough to have small, dying congregations. When I was at Wilmot, I sometimes only had 10 or 12 people in attendance. You spend a whole day preparing a sermon, like I was taught at Asbury Seminary, and then you preach it to the same dozen people Sunday after Sunday, well, it's discouraging."

"Small churches have their charm, though," said Pastor Snider. "Up in St. Louis, at Bethel, I had over 500 members, maybe 300 in attendance on most Sundays, and 600 or more for Easter and Christmas Eve. That was hard work. I'm glad to be here at Zion."

"Well, we're not in retirement yet," replied Reverend Nelson. "But I can see how it would be a welcome rest."

Pastor Snider wondered if this was a subtle dig at his age but decided to let it go.

"So," I said, changing the subject. "Usually when I'm in town, I'm hanging out with my crazy, mountain mad scientist friends. But since they were all either out of town or unavailable, and Pastor Snider invited me to join him, I came on over. Besides, couldn't miss Edna's pancakes."

They all agreed about the pancakes but wondered about my friends.

"Who are these 'mountain mad scientists?'" inquired Brother Hopkins. He was a graduate of Hannibal-LaGrange college up in northeast Missouri and had the largest church in town, maybe 200 or more members.

"Well, there's Steve Smith, a clinical psychologist who retired from the mental hospital over in Farmington. And Ed Tyree, who used to be a physics professor at Missouri State. And Mike Murphy, the state biologist. Then there's Carl Tyree, Ed's cousin. He's a journalist up in Jeff City.[3] Obviously not a scientist. And Ian Frisco, who teaches math at Derry County High School. And then there's Allen Adair, who's the principal at Derry County Junior High."

Brother Hopkins nodded. "I know Ian and Allen. They're members at First Baptist. Don't know the others."

Reverend Nelson chimed in. "Mike comes to First Methodist from time to time. His wife Nora's parents were Methodist missionaries to Kenya. She's there every Sunday she doesn't have to work. But I don't know Ed, Steve, or Carl. They from around here?"

"Not that I know, though there are a lot of Tyrees around these parts." answered Brother Hopkins.

"Well," I said. "Steve's from over by way of Kansas City originally. But Ed and Carl are from here. Carl lives in Jeff City, like I said. Ed moved here when he retired from Missouri State. He inherited his mom and dad's farm out by Low Wassie Spring."

"Now I do recall them," said Brother Hopkins, nodding. "His mom and dad would come to First Baptist for Christmas and Easter, maybe a baptism, wedding, or funeral. But Ed, no, I don't remember him."

---

[3] That is, Jefferson City, the state capital of Missouri.

"Well, he's a bit of an agnostic. Good man though," I replied. "Loyal friend. Honest. Hardworking. Takes care of his cows real well."

"That's worth something," Brother Hopkins allowed. "But he needs to repent and confess Jesus as Lord and Savior. Otherwise . . ." He left the rest unsaid but understood. The other pastors more-or-less agreed in principle with him, though they all added that Ed needed to be baptized as well.

"Well, baptism's mighty important," responded Brother Hopkins, "though not the way you boys think. 'You must be born again,' said Jesus in John chapter 3. Doesn't say a thing about baptism."

"Ah, but Jesus also said in Mark 16, 'Those who believe and are baptized will be saved,'" replied Pastor Snider.

"And Peter, on the day of Pentecost, said, 'Repent and be baptized, every one of you, in the name of Jesus Christ for the forgiveness of your sins. And you will receive the gift of the Holy Spirit.'" Reverend Nelson added.

Wanting to prevent a theological debate, I inserted myself into the conversation. "Say, you ever heard about the bad drought in Derry County back in '53? It got so bad that the Baptists were pouring, the Lutherans were sprinkling, and the Catholics were issuing promissory notes."

They all laughed, even Brother Hopkins. It wasn't true, of course, but there's nothing like humor to diffuse a situation.

"So, pastors, how often do you meet, and what do y'all talk about when you get together?" I asked.

"We meet every month. At the Riverside, of course. Mostly we talk about some struggles we're having, and we encourage each other. Even pray for one another. It's a good, edifying time," answered Pastor Snider.

"We also tell stories about our churches and denominations. Nothing confidential, mind," said Father McCready. "Often funny ones."

"Like what?" I inquired, hoping to hear some things I could put in the book I'm writing about life in Derry County.

"Go ahead, Father. You're the one who brought it up."

"I don't know if this is true, though Father Augustine Randall swore it was. He's a priest in the Diocese of Little Rock. A couple of years after he was ordained a priest, he was sent to Holy Family Catholic Church in Ft. Smith, Arkansas, to be their new pastor and to replace an old priest (don't remember his name—been there for years) who was retiring.

"Right after his first mass, Father Augustine felt there was something wrong. The people were restive. He couldn't figure out why. His sermons were pretty good, he thought. After all, he won a prize for preaching at seminary. He knew he was celebrating the mass well. And since his first mass he'd visited all the homes of the parishioners. They received him politely enough, but he could sense a little coldness towards him.

"One day, the chairman of the parish council came to visit him in his office. 'Say, father, didn't they teach you about the liturgy and how to do the mass at seminary?'

"'Of course,' he said, 'We had hours and hours of instruction and we all said practice masses, and the bishop was always there at our first masses once we became priests to make sure we can do a good job.'

"'Well, they must be doing something wrong there.'

"'How's that?'

"'Come on, everyone knows that right after the oblation, and every so often after that, you're supposed to clang the chalice on the radiator.' (It was an old church and had those old fashion radiator heaters.)

"Father Augustine couldn't believe his ears. 'What? I don't know what you're talking about. I've never heard about that before.'

"'Well, you talk to our last priest, and he'll set you straight.' And with that, he turned on his heels and left the office.

"As you can imagine, Father Augustine was confused. So, he called his predecessor. They exchanged pleasantries, and then the old priest asked how things were going. Father Augustine said he was troubled and asked 'Father, what's all this about clanging the chalice against the radiator?'

"The old priest laughed and said, 'Well, Father, we used to have an old wool carpet in the nave and another one up around the altar. When I'd move along the altar rail, and when people came forward, we'd build up some static. When I gave them the chalice (once we started giving the chalice to the laity), they'd get a shock when their lips touched the chalice. I'd touch the chalice to the metal radiator every so often to discharge the static.

"'Later, we put a new synthetic carpet in the nave and removed the one up at the altar all together. No more static. But the parish and I were so used to me clanging the chalice I just kept it up. Back then they knew the reason for it but, as the old parishioners died off, and new folks came in, particularly those from other denominations, they just assumed it was a part of the liturgy.'"

The pastors and I laughed heartily.

"Old practices often become *di rigore*," commented Pastor Snider. "Tradition, you know."

"Well, we don't have that particular problem in the Baptist Church, of course," said Brother Hopkins. "We use the little plastic cups which we pass down the aisles in trays along with the communion bread, you know, those little saltine-like things. No static there. But we Baptists have our own 'traditions' that can work out bad, sometimes."

We looked to Brother Hopkins.

"Well, come on. Tell us one ," I requested.

"This actually happened to me about 15 years ago. I ran into Bob Johnson at the Super Save. Haven't seen him in ages. He was an old man then, so he's probably gone on to be with the Lord. He was a deacon at First Baptist in Wilmot. Knew him since I was a boy.

"So anyhow, he says 'Howdy, preacher. Didja hear ol' Brother Kenny Ethelridge died?'

"I said I hadn't and that I was sure sorry to hear it, and Brother Johnson said that since Brother Ethelridge was beyond 90 and had been sickly for some time, it was a mercy. That being so, I agreed with him.

"Brother Ethelridge had been the pastor at First Baptist in Wilmot for years and years. When he retired, he stayed on in Wilmot and took on a small little country church, just preaching on Sundays, until he lost his eyesight. Then he and his wife moved in with his daughter over in Springfield.

"Well, Brother Johnson asks, 'Say, you comin' to his funeral? It's this Saturday at 11 o'clock. Ah know his family would be right glad to see you.'

"I said I'd have thought they were going to bury him in Springfield, but he said no, there was a family cemetery way back in the woods, south of Derry Creek, down towards Clarke's Hollow. Only a seldom-traveled dirt road back to it. Folks only go back there on Memorial Days to clean the graves and when there's a burial."

The other pastors obviously hadn't a clue where this was. They hadn't lived in Derry County long enough.

I said, "I know where Clarke's Hollow is. Both Elsbeth and I have been there several times to explore the cave in the hollow. But there's so many little cemeteries back in those woods, unless it was your family's, I don't see how you'd know how to get there."

"Exactly," responded Brother Hopkins. "And that's going to be important in a minute.

"So anyway," he continued. "I said I'd come to the service (which, he said, was going to be at Spademeyer's Funeral Home), but not the graveside as it was too far out. I had too many errands and little jobs I'd been putting off and my wife wouldn't take kindly to me being gone for the better part of the day.

"Well, he said he'd see me that Saturday and I went on about my business. The day came for the funeral, and I went into Spademeyer's, looked around, and didn't see anyone I knew except the widow and a few folks from Wilmot. I guessed they were mostly family from over by way of Springfield. I said hello to the people I knew and decided not to bother Brother Ethelridge's wife. She was looking so frail and was surrounded by so many folks, I just hung back and took a seat towards the rear of the chapel.

"I guess the family brought their own preacher with them—I didn't recognize him. But he did a passable, actually, quite passable, job of it. Made the service more about the hope of the resurrection and the Gospel that Brother Ethelridge preached rather than about the deceased himself.

"When the funeral was over and folks were getting up to file by the casket for one last look and to say a word or two to the family (who was gathered up front), I decided to slip out the back and get on with my day. As I left the chapel and went into the foyer, there was Brother Johnson talking to Billy Spademeyer. You know him, don't you, Pastor Snider?"

"Yes," he replied. "The whole family attends Zion."

"Well, brothers," he continued. "As you may know, Billy is Wilmer Spademeyer's oldest boy and at that time he just come back from the mortuary school up in St. Louis. He was there for more than four years. Got a degree in mortuary science. Before that he was in the Army for, I don't know, six or so years, maybe more, so he didn't know me.

"I guess Wilmer was that proud of Billy that he let him run the show that day. He said good day to me as I was leaving and Brother Johnson said, 'Thanks fer comin', preacher.'

"Of course, I wasn't there for what happened next, but Brother Johnson later filled me in. As soon as Billy heard the word 'preacher,' he said 'Preacher? Preacher?' He went into the chapel and slipped quickly down a side aisle, motioning all the while to his assistants who were standing off in the shadows on the other side of the chapel. Folks were standing around talking. Billy came up quietly behind, closed the lid of the casket, and took out his little crank key and put it into the keyhole and sealed it up. The assistants then wheeled the casket out, in a hurry, dignified, of course, and put it in the hearse. Billy quickly ushered the family out into the waiting limos, and they hightailed out at a speed, well, not normal for such an affair. Apparently, in the rush, they left that poor preacher from Springfield standing there in the chapel. He was surely puzzled.

"Now, I need to explain something to you fellers. You've probably only buried folks either in the city cemetery or some of the bigger family cemeteries close by."

The other pastors nodded their agreement.

"Well, these little family cemeteries up in the hills, they may only have a burial three or four times in a generation, so it's expected that the pastor would know where his flock's graveyards are or at least find out from the family before the funeral and drive out to see if he could locate it. There's too many, way too many, of these kinda places in the hills for poor old Spademeyer to know them all, so he relies on the preacher to lead the procession there. Got that?"

They said they understood.

"Okay, so now, I was in the process of running my errands. I first went into the Mercantile to buy some paraffin for the canning my wife was fixing to do. When I came out of the store, there was the funeral procession, sitting in front of the store all lined up all pretty like, the hearse in the lead and the widow's limo next after. Since it was only a block or two from the funeral home, I thought maybe they'd just pulled over to wait on another family car.

"Then I went down the block to Providence Feed and Supply to buy five pounds of ten penny nails. As I came out, there was that procession again. I thought, 'Now, that's right odd. What do you suppose they're doing?'

"Then I got into my car to drive over to the Super Save to get some milk and such. When I pulled out, I looked in the rearview mirror and bless me if those folks didn't pull out and head the same direction. I thought it was just a coincidence and went on over to the store.

"I came out of the Super Save with a couple of bags of groceries and there they were again, lined right up along the street. As I started my car and pulled out, up they all came right on my bumper, practically. And then I realized, they were waiting on me because they thought I was the preacher for the graveside service and that I knew where the cemetery was (which I did not) and was leading them there. Can't imagine what they thought of my going 'round town and stopping at all those places.

"Well, brothers, I tell you for an honest truth, I surely did panic. Not knowing what to do, I just stomped on the gas, trying to leave them behind. But they were right up on me. I'd make a turn and they'd make the turn. I'd speed up and they'd speed up. I ran over the railroad crossing down by 5th Street, musta been doing over 45, and they did the same. Can't imagine what the poor widow or the family thought, bumping and rattling along. Sure hope they had that casket latched down well in the back.

"I went around a corner where I knew they couldn't see me and ducked down that small alleyway behind Derry County State Bank, hoping I'd finally shake them off. I looked in the mirror and, sure enough, they drove right by the entrance to the alley, heading for who knew where since they themselves didn't rightly know.

"Brother Johnson said they went back to the funeral home. There was that poor old preacher, sitting on the porch in front of Spademeyer's with Wilmer. They got it all sorted, and Wilmer said he knew where the cemetery was as he buried someone there a couple of years back. He wanted to cuff Billy upside the head. Of course, it wasn't his fault. Well, not entirely. But eventually, they got Brother Ethelridge buried right and proper, and it all ended well."

We were spellbound as he sat musing for a moment or two. "You know," he finally said. "I bet that family had the most interesting funeral in Derry County for decades. Maybe a century. Folks still talk about it, now and again, and rib me for being the NASCAR preacher."

That broke the spell, and we all began laughing hard, tears running down our faces. Father McCready kept saying, "Oh, bless me, bless me." And Reverend Nelson got choked up and began to cough and Pastor Snider, hands all a-shake, tried to give him a drink of water but spilled it all over his and Reverend Nelson's shirts. That got them to laughing even more.

Well, you can know for certain that Edna came in to see what all the hullabaloo was about. We told her, in between further, tearful bouts.

"Well, Ah thought fer sure you wuz cryin'. Sounded fer all the world like the rapture had happened and you wuz left behind."

Father McCready looked up, puzzled. Pastor Snider said, "Never mind, Father, never mind. It'd take too long to explain."

Satisfied that we weren't dying or left to languish in the Great Tribulation, Edna left, but not before refilling our coffee and handing us a towel.

"You boys made the mess, you kin clean it up."

When our laughter died to the occasional guffaw, Pastor Snider said, "Well, maybe I should tell a funeral story myself, but make it a bit more somber to settle us all down."

"Alright, Pastor," said Reverend Nelson, "Be a killjoy. Just make sure it's interesting."

"Oh, it'll be interesting, sure enough."

"This was the worst and best funeral I was ever involved with. It was for a retired Master Chief Petty Officer. I won't mention his name, his family still being around and all. Alastair, being a retired Naval officer, can tell you, that's a pretty high rank."

"Highest enlisted rank in the Navy. It means he was the best of the best, top one percent," I replied.

"Well, not only was he a Master Chief, but he was a boat commander on the Mekong River during the Vietnam War. Swift boats, I think they called them."

I whistled in appreciation. "Man, those guys went through hell and back and made that round trip several more times again. That was brutal."

"Right. Did two tours, he told me, and won two Bronze Stars, a Silver Star, and a Navy Cross. Yet, he never got wounded, not even once."

I shook my head in disbelief. "What? That's incredible!"

"You're right, Alastair, it beggars belief. But he chalked it up to one thing—the Providential care of his Savior. He was a devout man, a little course around the edges—he was retired Navy, after all. A Christian first, a family man second, and a through and through, genuine American hero third. His folks were from Carondelet up by St. Louis, and the whole family attended Bethel Lutheran. Had for generations.

"He served for thirty years, retired, and went to St. Louis University on the G.I. Bill. Got a degree in math education. He was always good with numbers. Taught in inner-city schools and the kids respected him. He did that for about 20 years and then retired from teaching.

"Now, he'd been a smoker all his life. Started it in the Navy, he told me, and was never able to give it up. He also had a tendency every so often to drink a little too much beer. His kids said he was never a mean drunk, just a loud and friendly drunk. But he would never drink and drive, and he never abused his kids or his wife. For that matter, he didn't even kick the dog."

"Sounds like a good Lutheran," said Brother Hopkins, with more than a hint of sarcasm and disapproval.

"Well, Brother John, Luther said if you're going to sin, sin boldly. But I'd hardly call this bold sinning. And given the hell he went through in Vietnam, I think he deserves more than a little Christian charity."

Brother Hopkins, to his credit, was genuinely chastened. "You're right, Pastor Tom. I'm sorry I said that. Please forgive me."

"You're forgiven, but none's needed really. We all forget what it means to never judge a man unless we walk a mile in his shoes."

He continued. "So, naturally, he had a bad heart and, sure enough, he had a massive coronary and died. Seventy-two, a young man, at least by my way of thinking.

"His kids, who were all adults by then, of course, wanted to have a Lutheran funeral. But his wife said no, and, as the widow, she had the final say.

"It seems a few years before, under the influence of a friend, she had joined some kind of legalistic sect. I guess they are Christian, after a fashion—they do baptize with water in the name of the Trinity. Anyway, her new church told her that Lutherans weren't really Christians. 'They baptize babies and that's a heathenish Roman practice. And they believe you're saved strictly by grace through faith and say good works are unimportant, even wrong, and that's just damned licentiousness. And the Lutheran church was named after a man and not Jesus Christ and that's just a tradition of man and not the Gospel.'"

"Even I can see that's unfair," said Brother Hopkins. "Don't agree with baptizing babies, obviously, but the rest is pure poppycock."

"Yes, I'm afraid it was my lot that branded them "Lutherans." We know now that Luther just wanted to reform the Church, not leave it and start a new one," added Father McCready.

Pastor Snider thanked them both for their words and continued. "So, the Master Chief's funeral was held in this graceless church, at the mother's insistence, but the kids asked that I be there to say a prayer or two, at least for the deceased and them.

"I went to the funeral. Didn't wear my collar, I didn't want to offend. The church was completely devoid of any kind of decoration. The casket was set out at the front of church on a plain bier, no pall on it (that's a colored drape you put on caskets, Brother Hopkins), no drapes around it. And no flowers—they wouldn't allow it. Said the Bible didn't say a thing about flowers in church. And, perhaps worst of all, there was no flag on the casket as there should be for a veteran, which you would expect if there's not a pall. Guess the Bible doesn't say anything about flags neither.

"The attendance was rather small—just the kids and some of the older grandkids. The widow, of course, was there, and next to her was seated another woman. I assumed it was her friend. Such a sour-dispositioned woman I've never seen before or since. Every time she looked at the kids, grandkids, or me, she made a face like she was baptized in bad vinegar.

"The widow was crying, naturally enough (as were the kids). And every time she broke down, her so-called friend just said, 'Hush now, hush. Don't you be crying over that old sinner.' And she'd turn and glare at the kids and grandkids who were crying as well.

"The service started with a couple of Gospel hymns whose lyrics were completely out of place in that setting. Then, bless me, if the meanest man I ever saw stood up to conduct the funeral. He was stern faced, as if he were an Old Testament prophet confronting the worshippers of Baal. A tall, rail-thin man, he was dressed in a black suit, white shirt, black tie, and all out cruelty.

"I looked over at the family to see how they were doing. They seemed to be holding up as well as they could. I was delighted to see that sitting in the back of the church was a Navy honor guard detail. They were smartly dressed in their navy-blue dress uniforms and sat in quiet attention. There was a lieutenant in command.

"Well, this minister mentioned the Master Chief's name and the widow's name and then proceeded to catalog the deceased's sins. Drinking, smoking, cursing, and so on. The small sins of a great man, I thought. Nothing was said about his Christian faith or being a teacher in the inner city. And the only mention that man made of his service to his country was 'And no doubt he went whoring around while he was in the Navy.' He then looked pointedly at the honor guard detail, disapproval written all over his features.

"I looked back at those fine men and women. They sat there in professional attention, but they all looked grim and more than a few had scowls on their faces. The minister actually looked a little delighted, probably thinking he had discomfited them. Just shows how little he knew.

"Well, except for the seamen, the minister, and that worthless friend, everyone was crying. I confess to shedding a tear or two myself. Her friend kept saying, 'Hush, now. Hush yourself.'

"The minister concluded with, 'Well, there's nothing we can do now. We all know where this sinner is.' At that, the widow let out a wail, and, believe it or not, that pitiless woman beside her actually pinched her hard on her arm.

"The minister continued, 'Nothing we can do except pray for this poor grieving widow. And also pray that her unbelieving family will see the light and leave that Romish cult called Lutheranism.' Here he looked at me, gloating. I guess he knew, somehow, that I was a Lutheran pastor. 'And repent of their wickedness and see the true light.' And with that, there was another hymn sung. I guessed the service, such as it was, was winding to a close."

We had been mostly looking down at our coffee cups so far, but we all looked at the pastor now. His face was covered with fierce anger, as though he was actually back there at the funeral. Then his face softened, and he made a small smile.

"I heard a stir in the back. A soft command, the sound of people rising in unison, and another soft command. Down the aisle marched the honor guard, the lieutenant in the lead, ready to take the casket out of that God damned so-called church. When they got to the front, the minister moved to stop them, but a tall, muscular young seaman politely but firmly shouldered him out of the way. Boy, did he look angry and confused.

"At a word from the officer, they quietly lifted the casket from the bier, and, at another quiet order, they silently carried the casket down the aisle. The way they gently handled the casket, moving as one, you'd have thought they were carrying the most precious thing in the world. At that moment, it certainly was.

"When they left the building, there was a hearse waiting. The funeral home people greeted the honor guard with sad smiles. They probably overheard the service from where they had been standing in the foyer and were glad that someone was there to honor this heroic Christian man. When they got to the back of the hearse (its doors were open of course), one of the people from the funeral home got out an American flag and handed it to the officer. He and another seaman—his uniform was a bit different, I think he was a chief petty officer—anyhow, the two of them unfolded the flag, and, as the casket was slid into the hearse, they draped the flag in stages, covering the casket as it went in. It was the neatest bit of work I've ever seen.

"Those young men and women then marched to their gray Navy van, got in, and the van joined the funeral procession to the city cemetery. He should have been buried with his family at Bethel.

"When I arrived at the graveyard, the honor guard was already there. They came marching up to the hearse and retrieved the casket. I noticed, off to the side, there was a party of seven men and women armed with white rifles and another who held a bugle.

"The casket detail brought the casket from the hearse and laid it on the framework over the grave, assisted by the funeral director. Then they marched off to the side. The director ushered the widow and the family to the canopy and seated them. Her blasted friend tried to join them. The funeral director went over to her, and I overheard him saying, 'Ma'am, the family has instructed me to tell you that you're not welcome here and asked that you leave.' I guess the kids decided they were in charge now. She left in a sour-faced huff.

"Meanwhile, it seemed that three of the grandkids, big boys—I know one of them played football for Mizzou[4]—were blocking the minister's way to the graveside. He protested, but the boys were having none of it. They were talking quietly at first, but then the minister started to shout. The football player cut him off. 'Now, you listen to me, you mean son of a bitch. You get your scrawny ass out of here or grandpa won't be the only one lying in a grave.' Well, you can bet he scurried out of there quickly. He jumped in his car and sped out of the cemetery like the devil himself was after him. Maybe he thought he was."

We looked up again at this unexpected language. We were taken aback to see a look of quiet triumph, of exaltation even, on his face. There was a light shining in his eyes of pride and gratitude.

"Oh, thank you, God, for those young men and women. Thank you, Lord," he said softly.

He took a sip of coffee, probably cold by now, and continued. "Well, the widow heard none of this. She was too busy wailing and grieving over her husband, whom she was sure was burning in the fires of hell. Poor misguided soul.

"The oldest son came to me and asked quietly, 'Pastor, you knew dad, you were his pastor. You've known our family for years. Would you please say a few words?' I said I would. I went to the head of the casket and said the graveside service from memory."

---

[4] University of Missouri

A light came into Pastor Snider's eyes as he recited a portion of the liturgy.

"Into your hands, O merciful Savior, we commend your servant. Acknowledge, we humbly beseech you, a sheep of your own fold, a lamb of your own flock, a sinner of your own redeeming. Receive him into the arms of your mercy, into the blessed rest of everlasting peace, and into the glorious company of the saints in light. Amen.

"After I pronounced the benediction and made the sign of the cross, I stood back to let the honor guard perform their duties. The lieutenant took my place and turned to the firing party and nodded. The chief petty officer gave the command, and they began the salute, seven rifles, three volleys each, 21 guns. Well, we all jumped at the first volley, you always do, even if you're prepared for it.

"Then the bugler played taps. The officer and the petty officer saluted, the firing party stood at present arms. They did it, oh, so smartly, as he played. Being a veteran, I joined them in saluting. There were others there who saluted as well. I think we were all crying, but I noticed a slight smile on the widow's lips amidst all the tears. Maybe she had hope now, I wasn't sure.

"When taps were finished, the firing party and the bugler continued to stand at attention. The casket detail lined up alongside and began the time-honored duty of folding the flag. Brothers, I've seen many a military funeral, and I've never seen it done so well. When they were finished and the flag was perfectly folded into a triangle, one of the sailors presented the flag to the officer, who saluted the flag before he took it. When he had it in his hands, the sailor saluted, then stepped back in place.

"The officer turned to the widow and said, 'Ma'am, on behalf of the President of the United States, the United States Navy, and a grateful nation, please accept this flag as a symbol of our appreciation for your loved one's honorable and faithful service.'

"Ordinarily, that would be that, but he continued, his words were like wind blowing away a cold fog. 'He was a hero ma'am. A true hero. He won the Silver Star. He won the Navy Cross, all while fighting in the Vietnam War. He deserves all the honor my sailors can provide and so very, very much more.' He then rendered a slow, stately salute.

"Well, the widow had the biggest smile, now. Sure, there were tears on her cheeks. But she seemed as one who had awoken from darkness and went out into the light. She looked at the lieutenant and said, 'Thank you, young man. Thank you, thank you, thank you. Please give your men and women my thanks.' She then looked over at me and said, 'Thank you, pastor. Oh, God, thank you.'

"I walked over to her, gave her a brief hug, and said, 'You're so welcome.'

"As the honor guard filed out, I followed them. I introduced myself to the lieutenant and thanked him. I extended my hand, and he shook it warmly and assured me that what he and his men and women did was but the least they could do for the Master Chief.

"The chief came up, said hello, and we shook hands as well.

"'You know,' I said, 'you and your sailors saved the day. That was a horrible funeral.'

"The petty officer nodded and said, 'Well, it was a close thing.'

"I looked at him, puzzled, and said, 'How so?'

"'Some of the seamen were ready to rifle butt that preacher to death. Said the man was pure evil, not recognizing what the Master Chief had done for him, not being thankful for the freedom he enjoyed. I told them, 'Guys, we're here to represent the U.S. Navy, in fact the entire country. We're here to honor the Master Chief. We're not going to stoop to the shit-level lowness of that so-called minister, begging the pastor's pardon, sir.'

"I laughed and said, 'Think nothing of it,' shook their hands again, and headed to my car. The oldest son intercepted me and gave me the biggest hug.

"'Thank you, pastor, thank you. You don't know how much this means to us. We'll be there at Bethel this Sunday and we're bringing mom, whether she likes it or not.'

"'Oh,' I said, 'I think she'll like it. I think your father's death may have opened her eyes.'

"The son said that he hoped so and then he paused.

"'Pastor, it's too late to do anything about it now, but can we rebury dad at Bethel, with the family?'

"'Of course,' I said. 'No trouble at all. If memory serves me, there's plenty of room left where your family is buried.' They reburied him at Bethel the following month. The only time I've ever done a graveside committal over the same person twice.

"The widow did come back to Bethel. I'm sure her former friend and that minister cursed her soundly. She's buried next to her husband now."

He stopped and looked off into space. "You know," he said, "I've always enjoyed ministering at a military funeral. I love those young people, so full of life, and duty, and honor. Wish we had more like them."

He sighed, but it was a happy sigh, and said, "So, like I said, the worst and best funeral I've ever been involved in."

We sat there in silence for a few minutes and then Reverend Nelson said, "Wow, there's no way I can top that. Can't even get close."

We agreed, but still demanded that he tell us something.

"Yeah, you can't back out on us now. No matter how bad, you gotta tell us a story," said Pastor Snider.

With that particular man's insistence, the Methodist pastor groaned and said, "Well, I was going to tell the story about my first service here at First Methodist. The district superintendent and my mom and dad and brother were all there.

"Things went pretty well until there was the awfullest commotion in the choir. Old Mrs. Allen," he chuckled and continued. "She sings 'at' alto. You know the difference between singing something and singing 'at' something?" We all knew only too well the dissonant, out-of-tune screeching that comes when somebody sings "at" something.

"Well, it seems halfway through the choral anthem the top plate of her dentures came flying out of her mouth and hit Dee Dee Anderson, one of the sopranos, on the top of her head. Dee Dee was singing the descant and was going up for a high note when bang, a slobbery set of false teeth hits her head, tumbles down her face, the front of her choir robe, leaving a slimy trail, lands on her brand-new Jimmy Choos, and bounces to somewhere under the sopranos' row. Dee Dee was frantically wiping off the saliva on her face, the front of her robe, and on her shoes with a tissue. She smeared her makeup so much she looked like Tammy Fay in a hard rain. Mrs. Allen was scrabbling around on the floor looking for her teeth. 'I just got them!' she wailed. 'I paid $1,500 for them!' Dee Dee paused her self-rescue attempts and said, 'Well, you obviously paid too darn much if they won't stay in your dang mouth!'

"Needless to say, that was the end of the anthem. The service limped along as best as it could. Afterwards, one of the church council members came up to me and said, 'Reverend, welcome to First Methodist. Most Sundays we don't spit dentures at one another, but you never can tell.'"

At that we all laughed heartily and got up to pay Edna.

"Thanks, Reverend Nelson, for lightening the mood," I said.

"All in a day's work for a Methodist minister, Dr. Spring. All in a day's work."

The Rain Came Tumblin' Down

A Shape-Note Hymn Sung at Derry Creek Baptist Church

Father dear now did you hear,
The rain came tumbling down?
When the beasts embarked on Noah's ark,
The rain came tumbling down.
For forty days in all
The rain came tumbling down;
Till they came to rest on the mountain's crest,
The rain came tumbling down.

Mother dear now did you hear,
The sea came tumbling down?
On Israel's foe, that old Pharaoh,
The sea came tumbling down?
Moses led the people free, and
The sea came tumbling down.
Then Israel praised the Anci'nt of Days;
The sea came tumbling down.

Brother dear now did you hear
The walls came tumbling down?
At Jericho, with the bugle's blow,
The walls came tumbling down.
Seven times around they marched,
The walls came tumbling down;
Until at last with the trumpet blast
The walls came tumbling down.

Sister dear now did you hear
The roof came tumbling down?
When Samson's hands the pillars spanned,
The roof came tumbling down.

Philistines had blinded him;
The roof came tumbling down.
He made this prayer, "My strength repair!" and
The roof came tumbling down.

Son my dear now did you hear,
The giant came tumbling down?
When David threw the stone and slew
The giant came tumbling down.
Goliath taunted Saul and all,
But he came tumbling down.
Sword and spear David didn't fear.
The giant came tumbling down.

Daughter dear now did you hear,
The dark came tumbling down?
When Jesus died, the angels cried, and
The dark came tumbling down.
Down in the grave he lay,
The dark came tumbling down;
But 'twas God's plan for the Son of Man,
The dark came tumbling down.

Cousin dear now did you hear,
The gates came tumbling down?
When in hell he trod, the Son of God,
The gates came tumbling down.
O how the devil wailed, when
The gates came tumbling down.
Hell, death, and grave no more enslave,
The gates came tumbling down.

Neighbor dear now did you hear,
The stone came tumbling down?
O'er all His foes, the Victor rose,

The stone came tumbling down.
Christ is risen from the grave—
The stone came tumbling down. Now he's
raised on high, no more to die;
The stone came tumbling down.

It's an Adventure

"Pain."

"Pain?"

"Yep."

"Where?"

"Pretty sure it's everywhere."

"Nah, can't be everywhere."

"Yah wanna bet?"

I did a careful survey.

"Head?" No, it was okay. That's good, nothing worse than starting the day with a headache.

"Neck?" Hmm, a little sunburned, not bad.

"Shoulders?" Yeah, but not bad.

"Arms?" Likewise, a little bit.

"Back? Back? Hey, back!"

"What! Leave me alone!" Oh, yeah, the back was really sore.

"Hips?" A bit, like I wore a belt a little too tight.

"Butt?"

"Argh! Argh! Argh!" Okay.

"Legs?"

"Don't even talk about it." An incensed tone. "We don't want to talk about it. Do you understand, you Medieval torturer! Shut the heck up and leave us alone!" Wow.

"Knees?"

"Click, clink, clonk, clunk. And wait till when you go down the stairs, you bastard!" Err.

"Feet? Feet? Fee-eet?" No answer. They seem to tingle and burn but were mostly numb. Maybe that was a good thing.

What the heck was going on? Oh, I'm getting old.

"I'm getting old," I announced, to no one in particular, the "in particular" being the air and my wife, Elsbeth.

"Ohhh. Shush. Damnit. What time is it?"

I looked at the clock.

"5:30," I answered.

"5:30? 5:30! What are you doing up at this time of the night!?!"

"It's not night, it's 5:30 in the morning, and the sun's been up since at least, let's see, well, it's just come up. It's summer after all."

Up till now, she had kept her eyes closed, but now they popped open, glinting with a demonic glare.

"Now look here," she growled. "Either go back to sleep or get up and go to the kitchen and make yourself some coffee. And don't come back until 7:00 and bring gifts!"

"What kind of gifts?"

"Coffee made exactly the way I like it. And don't even begin to ask, 'How do you like it?' You know!"

She rolled away from me, determined to go back to sleep, but she stopped in mid-roll.

"Besides," she said, "You're not old, you're just stupid. Who else but a very stupid man hikes in the hills of the Ouachita Trail for 12 miles by himself?" She huffed, finished her roll, and went immediately to sleep.

"Must be magic," I mused to myself. "Could never get back to sleep like that."

I sat up carefully.

"Careful," my body said, in chorus.

"I am being careful," I groused, silently.

I stood up, slowly.

"Aaahhh!" my body commented.

"I agree," said I.

"What? Huh? Where…? Oh my God! Oh my God! Pain!"

"Now, you've done it, you woke up the feet."

I moved carefully to the bedroom door, trying hard not to stumble. I opened it, to be greeted by the two cats, a grey tabby and a tortoise shell. They looked at me with combined concern and scorn. Mostly scorn.

"Look, I told you he was an idiot," said the tabby. "Look at the self-inflicted pain he's in."

"Yeah," agreed the tortie, "But that's what he gets for not letting us sleep on top of him. Feed us!"

"That's right, feed us!"

Ignoring the two, I moved gingerly down the stairs into the kitchen, popped a K-cup into the machine, set a mug under the nozzle, and awaited the results, grabbing a couple of ibuprofen in the meantime. After a few minutes, I removed the steaming mug of coffee, inhaled its aroma, and took a careful sip. Okay, that's a good start.

After finishing the mug, I set it up for a second time, this one to drink leisurely as I read the news on my smartphone. I was starting to feel better, and the dialog with my body had receded to faint murmurs.

Finishing the second cup, I reflected on yesterday's hike. No, wait, it was not a "hike." It was an adventure, an endurance test, pushing the body, quickening the mind. I had covered 12 miles on the trail, with a succession of hills and valleys. What a challenge! I bet if you rolled out the hills and valleys flat, why, it'd be like 20 miles or more! Feeling pretty good about myself, I rose from the table with only a tinge of stiffness and made Elsbeth's coffee, exactly the way she likes it.

I entered the room at precisely 7:01 and said a cheery, "Good morning, baby!"

"Grrr."

"I made you coffee! Exactly the way you like it."

"Hmm. Okay." She sat up and reached for the proffered cup. She took a sip, then another, and then her eyes went from ill-tempered feral cat to something more or less human.

Taking another sip, she looked up at me.

"This is good. Thanks."

Setting down the cup on a coaster on the nightstand, she asked, "Why do you go on these hikes, anyhow? I'm mean, I get maybe four or five miles. Gets the blood moving and the thoughts flowing. But 12 miles?"

"Probably more, if you were to 'exalt every valley and make every mountain and hill low,'" said I, paraphrasing from Isaiah 40.

"Yeah, don't get biblical with me right now." She reached for her cup and took another sip. "Why? Why do you hike for such long distances? I mean, what about the pain?"

"It wasn't just a hike, it was an adventure, a challenge. There's always the risk of pain with an adventure."

I started to recall in my mind's eye some of the painful adventure experiences I had.

"Look," said Elsbeth. "If you're going to recall in your mind's eye some of the painful hiking experiences you've had, do it elsewhere."

"Adventures! Challenges! Not just hikes."

"Yeah, whatever, do it someplace else. I've got to get ready to meet with the pastor today to go over this week's music settings for the Eucharist and I don't want to be late because I was listening to your tales of daring-do."

I guess I've had "adventures" in the outdoors pretty much all my life. As a child, most of them were pain-free or pretty much so, injuries only consisting of the odd scratch, scraped knee, or cut finger. I have memories of climbing trees, building dams in streams, constructing forts, catching frogs and salamanders, dirt-clod fights, hiking with my family on weekends, and such. Before sending us outside, my mother would catechize my brothers and me with a series of questions (to which she would provide the answers, like "What do you do when you come to a street? Look both ways, right?") and send us out the door with the final admonition of the liturgy of mothers and children, "Be careful!" (A lot of mothers also added, "Have fun," but they were obviously from more liberal denominations.)

My first memory of a painful adventure was riding my tricycle down the sidewalk in front of my house on Ft. Leonard Wood. I was strictly enjoined to remain on that sidewalk and not to cross the road. When I came to where the sidewalk ended, I decided to continue, only to be surprised that there was a drop-off. It was probably only about four or so inches, but to me it seemed like a chasm. My mom, witnessing this in mid-catastrophe, came running toward me. As I went over the curb into the street, she said she heard me cry, "Be careful!" Not sure why I said that, must have been my religious training.

Shortly after graduating from Oakmont High School, my friend, Allen, and I went on a road trip to Colorado. We had a great time in the mountains outside of Colorado Springs and then decided to go to Estes Park where some friends of ours were staying in a family cabin. They had a really pretty daughter on whom I had a little bit of a crush. Allen, who was much better looking than me and who frankly didn't care much one way or the other about the young woman, naturally got all of her attention.

One day, Allen and I went to the Rocky Mountain National Park to do a short day-hike. We pretty much stuck to the established trails until we came to a swollen stream about seven or eight feet across. Ordinarily, hikers would cross the creek on some stepping-stones. But now the fast-moving water was three or four inches above the rocks, and I thought aloud that that didn't look much like the safest way to cross. I pointed to a tree which had fallen across the creek maybe 20 feet further downstream. "I'm crossing on that," I stated confidently. "You'd be an idiot to cross on those rocks."

Allen ignored me and jumped from stone to stone, getting soaked from the knees down in the process. I laughed at him, reaffirmed his idiocy, and began to make my way over the log. The first bit, still over the dry ground, was okay, but once I left the bank behind, my way was covered with a thick layer of moss, wet and slippery from the spray of the wild mountain creek. When I got to the center, well, I don't remember too much after that point, so I'll let Allen's account fill in the details.

"Yeah, when you got to the center, your feet began slipping and sliding all over and for a moment you looked like Wiley Coyote, suspended in midair, your legs just kinda kicking around. Ha-ha-ha! And then you landed, whump! Right astraddle the log. You said, 'Uuugghhh!' and rolled over sideways off the log into the creek. Ka-Ploosh! Hee-hee-hee! You floated downstream, face down, bubbles trailing behind you. Ho-ho-ho! I ran down to where you were floating, waded in and pulled you out. Ha-ha-ha-ha! And when I pulled you out, you came up sputtering and still saying, 'Uuuugggghhhh!' Hee-hee-hee-hah!"

Whether his rendition of the story is completely true, I couldn't say. What I can say is (1) I was thoroughly wet through, so I certainly fell in, (2) I moved pretty gingerly and sat down carefully for the next few days, and (3) I had never been so cold in my life. That water was from off the snowpack and barely above freezing. It was probably a good thing for my future wife's and children's sake that the water was so cold. Needless to say, Allen got a lot more attention from a certain young lady when he recounted this story than I got sympathy.

On most hiking adventures of the sort I'm describing, things happen so fast you really don't have much time to think. Wham! It happens. (You do, however, have plenty of time later to think about the pain.) But one of my more recent escapades gave me far too much time to ponder my predicament. I didn't enjoy it.

I was walking alone on a trail I've hiked dozens of times before near my house in Little Rock. I got about a mile into it and found I was miserable—I had waited too late in the day to start, and I was besieged by those tiny little mosquitos people in the South call no-see-ums. They were everywhere! Not having been bothered by them on previous hikes started earlier in the day, I hadn't brought either the bug net to drape over my hat or insect spray—gah!

I decided to call it a day, but I didn't want to retrace my way back, having alerted the tiny flying demons to my presence. The trail was on top of a bluff overlooking a small river. A side trail veered off from where I was standing which switched back and forth steeply down the bluff side to the river. If I took it, I could follow another path back to the trailhead. I had traversed it before and I knew it was a little tricky, and there were some shear drop-offs, but I was confident.

I started down and came to an awkward turn that required clambering over some rocks. It was overgrown with blackberry brambles and greenbrier vines, and it was difficult to see the pathway ahead. I stopped to consider. Deciding that maybe discretion and bug bites were the better part of valor, I turned to go back up the trail. The next thing I knew, my feet were sliding out from underneath me (despite good hiking boots), and I was flying head-down backwards off the bluff!

I landed in a dense bed of blackberries and greenbriers and stuck to them like Velcro. I did a quick body count and found I wasn't injured (at least that I could tell), but when I tried to rise, well, I wasn't going anywhere. Fortunately, I hadn't lost my hiking staff (four feet long, made of sassafras), so I reached behind me with the stick and pushed through the foliage to see if I could get a purchase. Nothing. I realized at this point that I was hanging in midair with nothing holding me up but the vegetation.

So far it held me up pretty solidly (as much as plants of the non-tree variety can be solid), so I was confident that if I didn't move suddenly I would be okay. For now. I lay there, considering my situation. The summer Arkansas sun was beating down on me mercilessly, but another thing I hadn't lost was my trusty olive-green fedora. It was still firmly seated on my head. I carefully pulled my right arm free and moved the hat to cover my face and continued thinking.

Out of the corner of my eye, just off to my left, and about three feet out of reach, I could make out a rock which, if I could grab it, would allow me to pull my way back on the path. I carefully ripped my left arm free of the thorns and tried shifting my body clockwise toward it. No good. I needed something to grab onto to make the pivot work. The only thing available were some good-sized, mature blackberry canes, really woody, and maybe the thickness of my thumb. I reached out and grabbed two or three of them. Argh! Those thorns really hurt! I persisted, pulling on the brambles, raising myself a little at a time, the sound of ripping clothing (not skin, I hoped) filling my ears with each move. After each short pull, I would have to settle back down again, reattaching myself, so as not to disturb my lofty, needley nest too much. Pull! Rip! Settle. Pull! Rip! Settle.

Finally, I reached the stone and laughed (and groaned) out loud and dragged myself to safety. I was covered with rips and tears and embedded thorns and bristles (which my wife, my daughter, and I spent the next two days removing), though I couldn't see most of it since I had landed backwards. Just my bleeding hands and arms, really. I was so pumped full of adrenaline that I couldn't feel a thing except elation at being alive.

As I headed back down the trail toward my car, the pain began, the pain of a thousand tiny punctures and cuts all over my arms, hands, and backside. When I got to the car, I reached for my phone to call Elsbeth. No phone. Somewhere lying under two or three feet of vines, or at the bottom of the bluff, was my smartphone. It was a good thing I didn't have to call for rescue.

When I got home, I reported this "adventure" to Elsbeth and my daughter (who was staying with us), my embarrassment overshadowing my pain. A chorus from a Greek tragedy responded to my tale.

"How many times have I told you . . . And why didn't you . . . I told you that . . . And here you are . . . You're gonna go and get yourself killed . . ."

I nodded meekly and submitted to having my shirt removed. Elsbeth held it in front of me, the fabric peppered with spots of blood.

"And look what you've done to your shirt . . . I don't know if I'll ever be able to . . . Don't you do this again!"

When I next hiked that trail, promising not to veer from the main pathway, I stopped at the point where that side trail branched off. I looked down over the side trail which zigzagged steeply to the river. It was completely covered with vines and brambles. I also saw what looked like a depression in the vegetation, maybe where I landed? There was nothing solid under that mass.

The Apostle Paul says, "In everything give thanks." Ordinarily, like all hikers, I would curse blackberry brambles and greenbriers. But now? "Thank you, blackberries. Thank you, greenbriers. Thank you, God."

It was a sign of God's providence that, in all these adventures, I never once broke a bone. Never, that is, until the fateful Cave River expedition.

The Cave, along with the Greystone and Marble Rivers, is a part of the National Park Service's Ozark Highlands Scenic Riverways. This river was famous, as you might guess, for the large number of caves which peppered the bluffs along the Cave River Valley, making it a veritable Swiss cheese of speleological adventures. Most of those are short, dusty passages, having dried up centuries ago. They were of no interest to the usual population of cave fauna and served mainly as summer and winter homes for timber rattlesnakes and copperheads. But some of them had very large rooms and long passageways, making them ideal for the adventurous caver. These were not the clean, concrete-paved caverns for tourists, but wild and untamed, the perfect place for an adventure for the trained and well-equipped caver.

Okay, I gotta take a moment to deal with a common misconception. Many people call folks who explore caves "spelunkers." That is not what we call ourselves. Instead, we prefer the title "caver." A "spelunker" is how a caver refers to an untrained, incidental visitor, totally unprepared, and often a victim of preventable injuries.

An oft told story amongst cavers about spelunkers goes like this. There were these two good-old-boys driving along a back road in their requisite, beat-up pick-up. One of them says, "Hey, looky thar, Luke, thars a cave over yonder."

"Yeah, Matt, let's check 'er out. Ah've got an ol' flashlight in the glovebox."

Pulling off to the side of the road, Luke gets out his flashlight (the batteries of which haven't been changed in the good Lord knows how long). They head over to the opening and slip-and-slide their way a few hundred feet into the darkness. About then, the flashlight goes out, leaving them in the pitch blackness of the eternal subterranean night.

"Don'tcha worry none, Matt," says Luke confidently, "Ah got me a perfect sense of direction."

So, they turn around, edging their way in the direction of the entrance (or so Luke thinks). Unseen to them, a substantial muddy pit lies in their path. They both fall in. And what do you think the sound they make is when they hit the water-filled bottom? "Spee-lunk!"

Alright, so back to our adventure. There was quite a party gathered at the National Park Service put-in after having been dropped off by the folks from Chase's Landing. There was the usual crowd of mountain mad scientists: Allen, Steve, Ed, Mike, Ian, and me. Joining us were Carl (the journalist from Jeff City) and Neil, my friend from Arkansas. Neil was an occasional member of our expeditions. He was a clinical professor of orthopedic surgery at the medical school in Little Rock. He was a person of dangerous enthusiasms. How dangerous? Well, his enthusiasms worried even Ed and Mike.

Setting out in four canoes, we lazily floated our way down the river, only working hard when we came to shoot some rapids or to avoid willow strainers.[5] We stopped at several points along the stream, tying up to a tree or rock,

---

[5] A "willow strainer" is a tree (often, but not necessarily, a willow) which had grown over or fallen into the river, its branches or roots allowing the water to pass through, but catching anything else that came its way. An unwary

getting out,t and hauling our caving equipment up the bank to the nearby caves. It was fun, but none of the caves proved difficult or especially large until we came to Dance Hall Cave.

Dance Hall was the location of a local speak-easy back during Prohibition. It had a large front room with a mostly smooth, clay-covered floor, perfect for dancing and drinking (probably Great Uncle "Cletus's" good stuff) during the summer when the cave was dry. It was summer when this expedition took place, but it was an unusually wet summer, and the clay, which extended several feet outside of the cave as well, was terribly slippery, making for dangerous footing.

After exploring the main room and reading the names and dates written in candle soot on the walls (many from my family), and checking out some side passages, we decided to head on down the river. About half of the crew were already at the canoes when I started back. It was a pretty steep slope, littered with large rocks, and covered with trees, and it was maybe 50 yards from the cave mouth to the river.

As I began to pick my way down, behind me I heard Neil say, "Whoa," a likely sign he'd slipped and fallen. I turned to see if he was okay. Next thing I knew, I was flying through the air! My feet must've slid out from under me, and I was hurtling down the slope. They say when such things happen, everything goes in slow motion. Well, that was true at first. I remember seeing a small tree. Oddly, I knew distinctly that it was a dogwood. I grabbed the tree to stop my descent. The dogwood said, "Oh no you don't!" I swung 360° and I continued my careening catastrophe until I landed with a resounding "Thwomp!" on a large, flat rock. I remember thinking to myself just before I abruptly halted on my

---

canoeist could get trapped therein and even drown if the current was strong enough. Willow strainers, far more than rapids, are the most dangerous obstacle in the river.

landing pad, "Tuck in your chin, keep your head off the ground. Don't want to get a concussion."

Perhaps because of this action, I still had a pretty clear head, and so I was able to take stock of my situation. My right leg was stretched above me, my foot being caught in the low branches of an oak. My left leg was bent at the knee underneath me. The remainder of me (except my head) rested fairly comfortably on my thoughtful, stony helipad. I wasn't in any pain. Yet.

Off in the distance, I could hear Neil crashing through the brush and yelling, "Don't move! Don't move!"

"Don't worry," I answered quietly. "I won't."

Neil appeared at my side and quickly began examining me with his surgeon's hands and keen eyes. "Well, nothing seems to be obviously broken." He gently prodded my abdomen. "Don't feel distension or tympany, at least not yet. Bet you've broken some ribs though." He and Steve helped me carefully down the remaining few feet and into a canoe.

"Good thing you tucked your chin like that, probably saved you a concussion or even a broken neck," said Neil.

"Yeah," said Ed. "When I heard you coming down, I looked up, and you were rolled up in a ball, just bouncing along."

"Yep," Allen joined in. "Looked like you did that sort of thing for a living, like you were a professional. Bet you could make good money in Hollywood."

Everyone laughed, including me. That was a mistake. Pain was finally rearing its gory head. Yes, I had certainly broken some ribs.

After pumping me full of ibuprofen and acetaminophen from his ever-present rescue bag, Neil and I set out with the others to continue our journey. I was glad the current was easy going as I'm not sure how well I could have paddled, even a simple I-stroke.

Well, the current was easy, for a while, and then . . .

The river forked into three branches. The center one was very shallow and went over two or three gravel bars, meaning getting out and portaging the canoes. The right side ran fast with at least one, maybe two, willow-strainers. Definitely a no-go. To the left, the stream was fast and deep and went around a bend past which we couldn't see. Generally, going with the fast and deep, providing you've got somebody good in the stern, was the way to go. Neil was in the stern, and he was very good with the paddle. So, a good 10 yards in the lead, around that bend we went.

As we rounded the curve, Neil and I saw something which froze our blood. Ahead, spanning the entire length of the branch, lay a huge sycamore, probably blown down in the last storm.

"Backstroke! Backstroke!" shouted Neil. We backstroked, slowing our progress so that we hit the tree with a modest bump.

"Draw stroke! Draw stroke!" Neil commanded. I gotta tell you, I was right glad I knew what a draw stroke was. For those of you who are ignorant of canoes and the paddling thereof, a draw stroke involves putting your paddle out at a right angle to the canoe about as far out as you can reach, the blade placed parallel to the canoe, and digging deep into the water. Then you pull back on the paddle, bringing it toward the side of the canoe. This moves it toward the direction of where the stroke began. When done in a coordinated manner and with strong pulls, it's a good way of getting over to the bank.

We were making good progress, with only about three feet to go, when . . .

The other three canoes came around the bend "hell bent for leather," as they say. Seeing the tree, but not Neil and me, their occupants did what most folks do in the face of impending disaster.

"Aaahhh!" yelled Steve.

"Oh crap!" agreed Ed.

"What the flying . . .?" added Mike.

"What's that damn tree doing there?" questioned Allen.

"Good God almighty!" opined Ian.

"Oh, Jesus!" prayed Carl. At least I think he was praying.

Steve and Carl, being in the lead of this group, slammed into the stern and then the left side of Neil's and my canoe, completely undoing our draw-stroking, tipping our gunwale upstream, and rapidly swamping our canoe. Neil and I quickly grabbed hold of the tree to keep from being swept underwater beneath it. Since I'm tall, I had the arm span to get a good hold, but Neil, off to my right and closer to the bank, was a good bit shorter and struggled to keep hold.

To my left I heard a great deal of sputtering and turned to see Ed desperately snatching hold of the sycamore. When he arrested his progress, I asked him, "You doing okay, Ed?"

"No!" he choked. I remembered that he was wearing rubber boots, which were, I'm sure, filling with water. I also noted he was not wearing a life vest. I was.

I turned to Neil and said, "Say, Neil."

"Yes?" he replied, with surprising calm. Gotta hand it to surgeons.

"I got this life vest on and there's about three inches of clearance between the bottom of the tree and the top of the river. Any reason why I shouldn't just let go?" I was equally surprised with how calm I was. I put it down to 23 years in the Navy.

"No, I can't see any reason why not." So, I let go.

The current swept me easily under the sycamore and brought me to within four or five feet of a gravel beach on the other side, barely 10 to 15 feet downstream from the tree. I clambered out of the water. Pretty sure I was unconsciously glad of how cold the water was, for I was feeling no pain.

I proceeded to grab paddles, coolers, and other canoe contents as they began popping out one after another from under the tree. Finally, a canoe, sufficiently full of water to float under the sycamore, came through. I waded in to snag it. What I didn't know was that Carl and Steve had managed to somehow go hand-over-hand along the tree to the bank, came up behind me, and jumped in to help. Steve waded up beside me. I was startled for a moment, but then we grinned at each other as though this was exactly the kind of adventure we had eagerly expected all day. But Carl, well, he grabbed a second canoe, couldn't hang on to it, and let it go. It slammed into the right side of the canoe Steve and I had, close to the stern, and pivoted our canoe towards us, fast.

Steve slipped and fell into the water, and the canoe ran over him, mere inches above his face. I was not so lucky. It crashed into my left side, my "my ribs are probably broken" left side. The pain was electric.

Thumping on my butt into the water, I didn't move until Ian and Neil (who eventually came under the tree as I had) very gingerly extracted me and set me down on a grassy area near the bank. Neil carefully opened my shirt and checked me over. Overlaying my already blackening bruises from my earlier audition as a stunt double were new sets of crimson weals and seeping abrasions. Neil clicked his tongue and said, "Pretty sure some of those ribs are broken. If not from before, I bet from just now."

"Thanks, doc," I wheezed.

Thank the Lord, the remainder of the trip was uneventful, and nothing was required of me except to sit in the bow and groan softly to myself.

When we got to the pull out, the gang insisted that I sit quietly in Ed's truck while they loaded the gear and the canoes. Neil and I rode back with Ed (we were staying with him), me continuing my groaning in the front.

"I don't mean to be rude, Alastair, but would you mind groaning out the passenger window? It's giving me the creeps." asked Ed.

I turned toward him and groaned insistently in his face.

"Some people are just that rude," noted Ed.

Later that evening, I showered, moving very carefully, and marveled at the technicolored display which was my body. Such an assortment of blacks, purples, blues, and reds. I knew these would be joined soon by yellows and greens. Neil examined me thoroughly and pronounced me free from serious injury.

"What do you mean by serious?" I groused. "This feels pretty serious to me."

"I mean we don't need to take you to the hospital tonight. Might want to get an x-ray or two tomorrow. You've definitely cracked some ribs, though. No defects, so you'll be okay for now. Not much more I can do. Man, you're gonna really, really hurt tonight. I've got some Tylenol with codeine in my rescue bag. Want some?"

"All you have and two more bottles besides."

Allen and Ian came over for dinner after they cleaned up. As we were sitting around in Ed's book- and taxidermy-festooned living room, waiting on steaks, we recounted the day's events. We all laughed (albeit, I did so very reluctantly and painfully).

"Well," I said thoughtfully, "I guess I gotta thank the good Lord that he was watching out for me today."

"You ask me," Ed replied. "Sounds like the good Lord's got it in for you."

As I chuckled to myself at this memory (thankfully without pain), Elsbeth came through the door, cheerily shouting, "I'm back!" She came straight into my office, knowing that's where I do most of my reminiscing. Under her arm was a church service book, loose sheets of music dangling from between its pages.

She looked at me and said, "Oh, good, you've finished recalling in your mind's eye."

"Yes, I have. And I had a good time, too!"

"Didja think about falling off the cliff into the briers and brambles?"

"Yes."

"And when you fell down the mountainside and broke your ribs?"

"It was only a bluff. A steep bluff, a long bluff, I'll admit, but only a bluff."

"And you still think these were adventures and not you just being stupid?"

"Yes, and I want to remind you that this is all a part of our family's rich heritage."

"How's that?"

I proceeded to remind her of an incident in England. I was at Oxford, doing my sabbatical, and the whole family went on a ramble through the Cotswolds on a weekend. My two sons, Aaron and Ben (eleven and nine at the time), were running ahead of us, darting in and out of the trees, jumping over partially fallen stone walls, and peering through the gaps at us, trying to startle us. On one such dash, Ben swerved suddenly to the left, disappearing behind a clump of nettles. We heard a "Whoa!" followed by a splash.

We ran up to where he vanished and looked through the newly formed gap. There, sitting at the foot of a hidden, water-filled ditch, was Ben, coughing and spitting water and mud out of his mouth.

"Are you okay?" asked Elsbeth with motherly concern. "Did you have an accident?"

"It wasn't an accident, mom," said Ben, picking himself up. "It was an adventure."

The Possum

"The Virginia opossum, scientifically known as Didelphis virginiana, is North America's only marsupial. As with all other marsupials, they give birth to very undeveloped young who somehow manage the trek to their mother's pouch (called a marsupium) where they latch on to a nipple and refuse to show themselves for anywhere from 75 to 120 or more days. Many do not survive the arduous journey and still others fail to find a vacant nipple. These young, of course, do not survive. To compensate for this high infant mortality rate, mother opossums give birth to litters as large as 20. (By the way, juvenile opossums are called joeys, as are all young marsupials. It seems that the Australians, having largely cornered the market on the mammalian infraclass Marsupialia, get naming rights.) Once they are weaned . . ."

"Hey, Dr. Spring, enough with the biology lesson. We know all about them critters. And we don't called 'em Virginia opossums or Didelphialass virginwhatsits. They're possums, plain and simple. So, get on with your story."

"Okay, okay. Well, possums are important members of the Ozarks' population of wild creatures."

"You mean critters, right?"

"Yes, okay, critters. Sheesh. Who's telling this story?"

"Well, apparently, not you."

"Ahem. Continuing on, Ozarkans will tell you that, when you cannot find any other game, a stewed possum, served with dumplings, makes a tasty meal. They will tell you that, but they do not mean that. What they mean is, if the choice is between facing starvation or possum, they will reluctantly eat the possum, washed down with a pint of the 'good stuff' to cut the grease."

"That's 'bout right. Nasty things, them possums are. Now get on with the story."

Quite a few years back, in my Navy days, my wife, kids, and I went to visit my mom and dad, traveling from NAS Millington to their home in Oakmont. As usual, my mom was waiting at the front door when she heard us pull up. With the biggest smile, she gave hugs all round, punctuated with her warm laughter, amid the happy and indecipherable clamoring of the grandkids. Noticing my dad's absence, we looked around the room for him. We found him sitting in a dark corner of the family room. This was odd—he was usually close by to greet us as well. On closer inspection, we saw him glowering at no one in particular and everyone in general with two very swollen black eyes.

"Dad, what in the world happened?" I asked.

"I don't want to talk about it," he replied

At this point, my mom, who is not one to laugh at my dad's expense, broke into a most ungrandmotherly cackle.

"You won't believe what happened!" she exclaimed.

Shooing the kids to the game room in the basement to play "poo' ball" on the billiard table, Elsbeth and I stowed our suitcases in the guest room, sat down at the kitchen table, and said, "Okay, Mom, what's this all about?"

Dad let out a groan, shifted his position in the chair, and continued his pout.

"Well, I tell you what, I thought for sure I had lost your dad to a heart attack or something," Mom said. "I was washing dishes and I heard an almighty scream coming from your dad's workshop. Sounded for all the world like a little girl. I ran down to the basement, went out to his workshop, and found him standing there with a black eye, yelling and shouting and hitting this possum on the floor over and over again with a 2x4."

She broke down into another laughing fit. When she finally settled down, she told the tale of what will always be known in our family as *The Possum*.

Just a couple of days prior to our visit, Dad was on one of his yard cleaning crusades. Using a rake, he had gathered up all the leaves, branches, weeds he'd pulled earlier, and other detritus, and dragged them into a large burn pile. He set the rake down and began looking for the gas can he thought he had brought down to set the refuse on fire. He realized he had forgotten it, so he turned to go back to the house and . . .

Well, the rake.

When we were growing up, dad had always told my brothers and me that if you couldn't find a tree or something to lean a rake against, you should always place it on the ground, tines down. Otherwise, you could step on the tines which would lever the pole right into your eye. Dad had forgotten this fatherly advice. He stepped on the rake. It did indeed hit him in the eye. Black eye number one.

Disgusted with himself, he threw the rake down and stalked up to his workshop to get the gas and some matches. When he went into shop, he noticed that there was some insulation hanging down from the ceiling in a corner (he didn't bother finishing the interior walls or ceiling—just put in some insulation to keep the shop warm). Selecting a 2x4 about four feet long from his lumber stash, he pushed up on the batting. To his considerable astonishment, out boiled a very irate possum who landed on Dad's chest and proceeded to do a pretty fair Cottoned-Eyed Joe on his flannel shirt.

If you've ever seen an angry possum, you know it's an intimidating sight, all spikey fur, black eyes blazing, and a mouth full of a ridiculous number of sharp teeth. Apparently, Dad didn't care for the varmint's dancing choice, and he knocked the possum to the floor. Thereupon, he began to bash the unfortunate creature with the aforementioned 2x4 over and over again, screaming and shouting all the while.

At this point, Mom ran into the workshop, saw my possum-assaulting Dad, and asked, "John, what in the world happened?"

Panting from exertion (and more than a little panic), he answered, "I don't want to talk about it."

Satisfied that he wasn't going to die, Mom shook her head and returned to the kitchen.

Dad surveyed the possum. It was lying on its side, tongue lolling, eyes closed, blood seeping from its nose and mouth, and liquid feces pooling around the anus. It gave off the most horrible stench. Satisfied that it was dead, he picked it up by the tail and stumbled toward the burn pile, spewing wrath and Valhallic imprecations like the collected curses of a dark pantheon of minor gods.

He tossed the possum into the pile and looked around to find the gas can. He had understandably forgotten it. Lashing the air with further profanities, he turned to go back to the shop and . . .

Well, the rake. Again.

He stepped on the upturned tines, and the rake joyfully rose to meet his face. Black eye number two. Filling the atmosphere with a verbal lightening of thunder god-like proportions, he tossed the rake into a nearby tangle of honeysuckle and brambles. (He later retrieved it; his frugal

Pennsylvania Dutch ancestry was too strong to abandon it all together.)

He stomped up to the workshop, grabbed the gas can and matches, and stalked back down to the burn pile and . . .

The possum was gone.

A possum's ability to play dead (to "play possum," as Ozarkans say) is well known. But this individual had the ploy down to a fine art. After scanning around for the animal, expecting to see it limping away, his hunt proved fruitless.

Disgusted with himself, the burn pile, the rake, and, above all, the possum, he decided to call the whole thing off, gathered his various implements, and slowly returned to the house, tears rolling down his face from his much-battered eyes. He went inside and threw himself down into a family room chair. Mom saw him coming in, now adorned with a second black eye.

"Well, John, what happened now?" she asked incredulously.

"I don't want to talk about it."

We sat in amazement as Mom finished her tale, our eyes moving back and forth between Mom and Dad.

"Well, Dad, are you okay?" I asked.

"And did you ever find the possum?" added Elsbeth.

"I don't want to talk about it."

Gimme that Real Ol' Time Religion

Pastor Tom Snider called me the other day, asking if I was going to come to my mom's home in Oakmont for Thanksgiving. I replied that I was and that Elsbeth and I were actually planning on coming over to Derry County for the weekend afterwards. We were going to check out some property down on the Cave River near the small town of Johnson Corners on which to build our home for retirement. We would be staying in a Bed and Breakfast at the old Muller's farm just outside "The Corners" (as many folks called Johnson Corners).

"Then I can expect to see you at Zion on Sunday?" he asked.

"Of course, looking forward to it," I answered.

"Say, you got plans for lunch on Saturday?"

"Well, no. We are going to drive into Providence that day to meet with the realtor. Elsbeth and I have an appointment at 2:00. I suppose she could spare me for lunch. She wants to go and check out the new antiques barn over at Wilmot and would probably be glad not to have me shuffling around morosely after her."

He laughed and said, "Well, you remember Brother John Hopkins, the pastor at First Baptist?"

I indicated I did.

"Well, his father's going to be in town. Most of the time he lives with his granddaughter in Columbia—she's a professor at Mizzou. He's coming down to Providence—the whole family's coming down, apparently—for Thanksgiving. Brother John thought we pastors would enjoy meeting him and talking about the real old-time religion here in Derry County. Evidently, he was a pastor at First Baptist for quite some time. He has a lot of stories."

"Brother John's father? Brother John's got to be, what, in his mid-70s, right?"

"Seventy-five last October. His dad is 96. Brother John told me his father's physical health is going down pretty steadily since he had a fall this past summer. But he says his mind is as sharp as ever. He thought we ought to hear his stories while he was still around."

"Well, I'd be glad to be there. Riverside at 12:00?"

"Make it 11:30. I've got to visit a new family that's just moved into town at 1:00."

"It's a date." I hung up and went to tell Elsbeth.

That Saturday, after dropping Elsbeth off in Wilmot, I pulled up into a parking space on the courthouse square. I was a little bit early, so I walked into the Mercantile to talk with Bat Simmons. We passed the time of day and then I told him I was heading over to the Riverside for lunch.

"Edna's not there today," said Bat. "Her hips got to botherin' her somethin' fierce after bein' on her feet all day Thanksgivin' and the day before. Jessica's rulin' the roost today."

I smiled. "She's your granddaughter, right? The one who lives in St. Louis? I remember coming into the Mercantile when she was a little girl. I guess she was in town for the summer. She'd sit right there at the register on a tall stool next to you and act like she was the queen of the store. And you'd treat her as if she was. You fairly doted on that girl."

He smiled back. "Yes, she was all pigtails and freckles back then. Had me fair wrapped 'round her little finger, so she did. All growed up now. Graduated from Washington University in St. Louis with a bachelor's degree in bizzness. Keeps tellin' me now as to how Ah need to get all computerized and such like. Ah don't know. Don't know that Ah kin cotton on to all that new-fangled technology." He paused, then continued, "But Ah reckon as how she'd be the one to get me to do it. Smart as a whip, that girl."

I laughed and bade Mr. Simmons good day and headed over to the Riverside. As I walked into the restaurant, I was greeted, as always, by the jingling bell. Behind the counter was one of the prettiest redheads I've ever seen. I knew instantly it was Jessica. No longer in pigtails, her red hair was cut in a very professional and becoming style. And while they had faded some over the years, she still had a liberal sprinkle of freckles on her smiling face. Her green eyes immediately lit up with recognition.

"Dr. Spring! It's so good to see you. I was hoping you might come by."

"Jessica, it's good to see you, too! Your grandpa told me you'd be here. I hear you graduated from Wash. U. Congratulations!"

"Thanks, and I want to thank you again for your help in getting admitted and getting that scholarship."

A few years back, knowing that I was a college dean and professor, and with the encouragement of her grandfather, Bat, she had emailed me asking for help with her college applications. I gladly assisted her, secretly hoping she'd come to school in Little Rock.

"Well, I was glad to help. You know, there's a good MBA program down at the university in Little Rock."

"Well, I just might check it out. Shame you don't teach in the College of Business, though."

"Yeah, well, teaching teachers is my thing. Anyhow, think about it."

She said she would and asked me if I was meeting someone. I said I was there to have lunch with Pastor Snider, Brother Hopkins, and Brother Hopkins' father.

"They're in the back, Dr. Spring. Why don't you go ahead and give me your order now. I bet I remember it."

While she was in high school and college, Jessica used to work at the Riverside during her summer vacations. She has a sharp mind, so I said, "I'm not going to take that bet. The usual, cheeseburger, medium, trimmings on the side, fries, and a Dr. Pepper." Elsbeth wasn't here, so I was going to indulge. Besides, as they say, "Best Burgers in the Ozarks."

"That's what I thought," she laughed. She gave her head a little nod which made her hair bounce delightfully. She went back to the kitchen to place my order. I watched after her, I hoped without being too much "in the flesh." I gave a wistful sigh over my departed youth and headed to the back. At the usual table sat Pastor Snider, Brother Hopkins, Reverend Nelson, and a very elderly gentlemen whom I assumed was Brother Hopkins senior.

As I joined them at the table, I said hello to them, expressed my delight in Reverend Nelson's being able to join us, and asked "Where's Father McCready?"

"He had to go over to Wilmot for a funeral," answered Pastor Snider.

Nodding my head, I turned to the older gentleman and said, "You must be Brother Hopkins' father. It's a pleasure to meet you, sir."

He was a frail looking man, at least physically, but his eyes twinkled with good humor and intelligence. I was surprised to hear him answer in a strong, clear baritone voice.

"Yes, sir, Ah'm Brother Thomas Hopkins, late of Derry County, but still a Derry County man through and through.

Ah was the pastor at First Baptist for nigh on 35 years afore handin' the charge to my son. Afore that, Ah was a revival preacher in these parts, and Ah picked back up that vocation when Ah retired from First Baptist." He stood up slowly and shook my hand with unlooked-for strength. "And Ah know who you be, young man, my son told me about you." I smiled at being called a "young man." "You're Dr. Alastair Spring and you teach teachers down in Little Rock at the university. A noble profession is that, and I'm right proud to meet'cha."

We both sat down, and Brother Thomas looked me straight in the eye and got to what, for him, was probably always the main point. "So, tell me, young man, are you born again?"

I answered him straight forwardly, "Yes, sir, I am. I am saved by grace through faith in Jesus Christ, the only Savior and Redeemer of the world. I was raised in the Baptist church, Southern Baptist, mind you. At nine years of age, I went forward at an altar call and shook the preacher's hand. Next Sunday, during the evening service, I was baptized."

"Well, you were raised right. Just a shame you had to backslide and become a Lutheran." He said this with a wink to me that I don't think the others saw. The other three clergymen shifted uncomfortably.

"Now, Dad," interjected the younger Brother Hopkins. "There's no call for that. Dr. Spring is a good, solid Christian man."

"Oh, well, Ah was just foolin' with him." He smiled at me, and I smiled back. The other pastors relaxed in relief.

"Well, Professor Spring," the older Brother Hopkins said. "Ah don't have the formal education y'all have. Ah did graduate from Providence High School, back when that was considered quite a high level of learnin', and Ah was well educated for the time. Learned my Latin and Bible, back when they taught such things, afore schools got so heathenish, and was at the top of those subjects. But Ah didn't go to college like my son. Gotta tell you, Ah was right proud when John went off to Hannibal-Lagrange College and prouder still when he graduated *summa cum laude*." He said those last words with the correct pronunciation, showing he did in fact know his Latin. I wondered how much of his hill folk accent was affected, but I guessed it was largely just habit.

"But, like Ah said," he continued. "Ah don't have the learnin' that y'all have. Ah'm what you call a self-educated man. Ah know my Bible and Baptist doctrine. But Ah also know my church history, and Ah know how much we owe to Brother Luther and his teachin' about bein' saved by grace through faith. Don't hold to that silly notion some preachers have in these parts that the Baptists are the original Church going back to John the Baptist. Ah appreciate my Lutheran brothers. Just wish they'd get rid of that foolish notion of baptizin' babies.

"But," he continued, reflecting. "Ah reckon as how we Baptists got a foolish notion or two in our teachin'."

Pastor Snider nodded. "We can't know the entire counsel of God, and we're all sinners saved by grace and grace alone."

"That's a fact," said the older man, and we all agreed it was so.

"So, Brother Hopkins, I understand you have some interesting stories from your time of active ministry. I'm a collector of such stories—I'm even writing a book on them and other goings-on in the Ozarks—and I'd dearly love to hear them."

"Lordy, Ah have no idea where to begin," he said. "But Ah reckon Ah kin tell a tale or two. Mind, my memory's not as good as it once was," he added.

"Probably the best stories were from the time when Ah preached at revival services or protracted meetin's, as we sometimes called them. We were purty ecumenical, as they call it now, in a good sense, mind—we all believed in the Gospel and were proud to call each other 'brother,' regardless of our affiliation. We especially preached a lot with Methodist ministers back then." He nodded to Reverend Nelson.

He sat considering for a moment, and then began.

"Back afore Ah was the pastor of First Baptist, Ah preached a lot at these revivals. We often have what they'd call brush arbor meetin's."

I indicated I knew what these were, but Pastor Snider and Reverend Nelson said they did not.

"Well, the way it worked was this. Folks'd find a nice level area of land, sometimes an acre or more. Some of the menfolk would come and clear out the weeds and bushes and such. Then they cut down some young pines. They'd trim the branches off some of them trees to make poles and erect a scaffold over the grounds. Yes, sir, sometimes they'd cover the whole piece of land, or most of it. Ah've seen arbors purty near cover an acre—it was a big to do, Ah'll tell you. Once the frames where in place, they'd roof it over with those pine branches and other brush they cut, to make a nice cool place for the meetin'."

"Ah, I see," said Pastor Snider. "Thus, a brush arbor."

"That's right," agreed the elder Brother Hopkins. "Let me tell you, brothers, that brush arbor was mighty handy 'cause most of these meetin's were held in the summers, usually toward the end of July and beginnin' of August, when the farmers had mowed their hay and the rest of their crops were a growin' and not near toward harvest yet. Each of them boys would take it in turn each day to go back to each other's farms to see to the livestock and make sure everthin' was all right.

"Anyways, this was always the big event of the year. 'Course, we were hopin' folks were comin' to hear the Gospel and get saved or rededicate their lives to Jesus. But we knowed that this was the biggest entertainment folks'd see for quite some time, at least till the Christmas pageants the schools and churches would have.

"This bein' so, the farmers would load up their wagons or, in later years, their trucks, with quilts, and pots and pans, and food, pile in the young'uns and their wives, and come set up camp near the meetin' grounds. That's why they were sometimes called 'camp meetin's,' don't you see?

"Some of the richer families'd have tents, but most folks'd drape a tarp from some trees, or over some left-over pine poles, or over their wagons, make a good stone fire ring with an iron stand for cookin', and have a grand ol' time. Not just attendin' to the preachin', mind, though that was the main thing, but also catchin' up with folks they might not've seen for months. This was mighty important and was part of the reason why these gatherin's might last a couple of weeks or maybe even upwards of a month."

We all let out appreciative murmurs.

"And nowadays, you can't hardly get people to attend a week-long revival meeting in a comfortable, air-conditioned church," reflected the younger Brother Hopkins sadly.

"That's about right, son," replied his father.

"As Ah said," he continued, "We was right ecumenical in those days and we'd have preachers of all kinds: Baptist, Methodist, and maybe even a Disciples of Christ or two. We'd take it in turns to preach our sermons. One brother'd preach for two hours in the mornin', another for two hours in the afternoon, and still another for two hours in the evenin'. Ah say two hours, though it was said we'd preach for two hours or when our voices gave out. And let me tell you, friends, it was a rare and sorry preacher who couldn't hold forth for longer than the assigned time.

"Back then, folks appreciated long sermons. They'd spread their quilts or blankets out on the grass, sit down as a family, and listen hard. Didn't have no TV back then and folks could sit and pay attention for a long while. People wanted their sermons long and also eloquent. Rhet'ric was important back then. A good preacher would hold forth on a Bible passage for a while and then commenced to tellin' stories and paintin' pictures, so to speak, and keep their assembly's attention. Folks'd hang on to every word. They especially liked to hear about how hot it'd get in hell for the sinner and how beautiful heaven was. And the hotter the flames and the more wonderful the streets of gold, the better they'd like it. They purely loved the story of Lazarus and the rich man or how in heaven we'd see all our long-gone kinfolks and how we'd shake each other's hands or hug on each other's necks. Well, that's what they'd wanted to hear, over and over. Didn't matter if all three preachers in the day said purt' near the same thing. They purely loved it."

Jessica came in with our drinks. We thanked her and looked back to Brother Hopkins.

First taking a sip, he continued, "So, with this in mind, let me begin, as they used to say, a-storyin' for you."

He sat for a moment, casting around in his mind as to where to start. Suddenly, his face lit up and he began. "One time, the field we're meetin' in was very level an' the folks in the back couldn't see the preachers none. Mind you, seein' the preacher was nigh on as important as hearin' him. Folks'd want to see that preacher stompin' and a thumpin' about, wavin' his arms and punchin' and flappin' his hands. And the stompier and wavier he was, the better the people'd like it.

"So, the brothers that built the arbor set about erectin' a kinda stage. They brought in some ol' planks and boards, and, my lands, such a sawin' and hammerin' Ah never did see or hear afore or since, Ah tell you for truth. It was maybe four feet high, maybe a little more. It'as right purty and worked mighty well. For a while.

"Now, there was this big ol' boy. Methodist preacher he was, and his name was John Elden. He was a circuit preacher, as they used to call 'em, meanin' he had three or four churches he'd preach at, rotatin' every week.

"Like Ah said, he was a big ol' boy, maybe six foot four or five. And must've weighed near 300, 350 pounds. Well, gentlemen, let me tell you, he could flat preach. When he talked about hell, it was hotter'n the sun, and when he talked about heaven, why, you could practically feel the cool breezes of Zion on your face.

"At this particular meetin', he was talkin' about how poor ignorant sinners'd get cast into the very depths o' the lake of fire. Said the very ground'd open up under their feet and swaller 'em whole.

"Well, he commenced to stompin' around and wind-millin' his arms, sweat all a runnin' down his face and him a moppin' it up with a big, red bandana. He was flat out yellin' an' askin' folks, 'Y'all want the ground to open up under you?'

"'Lord, no!' they'd shout.

"'Y'all want to be pulled down into that lake o' fire and burn, Burn, BURN, brothers and sisters?'

"'Lord, no! Save us, Jesus, save us!'

"About then he gave a mighty stomp of his right foot— remember it as if was yesterday. Like Ah said, he gave a mighty stomp and . . ."

He smiled, then broke into a chuckle, then a hard laugh. We joined him just out of the pure joy of it.

"And then, them boards under him broke to pieces, and down went Brother Elden through the stage, like the ground'd open up and the gates of Hell was drawin' him in.

Well, people started a shriekin' and a shoutin'. 'Save us, Lord Jesus! Save us, O, deliver us, Jesus, Jesus, Jesus!' They figured if even a good man like Brother Elden'd get snatched down by ol' Scratch,[6] what hope'd they have?

"Well, in a little bit, we preachers, standin' off to the side, cottoned on to what occurred, an' we went an' hauled him out o' there. Let me tell you, that was some undertakin'. Took four of us to get him out o' there and we got mighty tired an' sweaty a doin' it. Ah tell you for truth, though, he did look mighty comical, him sticking out from the floor o' that stage at about chest high, bein' mighty consternated with it.

"Well, did that stop him none? No, it did not! Once we pulled him out, he went right on a preachin'. Didn't trust that stage none, so he commenced to stompin' and a roarin' around the folks, goin' out at 'em like.

"'Did you see that?'

"'Yes, Lord!'

"'Did you see that?'

"'O, Lord!'

"'Did you see THAT?'

"'Jesus, save us!'

"'That's how fast the gates of Hell kin suck you in and swallow you UP! That's how fast the jaws of the Devil kin chew you UP! That's how fast them ol' demons kin scrabble up from the depths of Hades and pull you DOWN!'

"'Jesus, Jesus, Jesus, O, Lord, save us, save us!'

"Well, gentlemen, we preachers were purely amazed at this man. The anointin' was on him somethin' powerful. We could almost see the fire of the Holy Ghost upon him, and we began a shoutin' too.

"'Amen!'

"'You preach it, brother!'

"'That's right, you go right along there!'

---

[6] An Ozark nickname for Satan. Others include "ol' Slewfoot," "the ol' gentleman," and "ol' Hobb."

"'Ain't it so, ain't it so!'

"'Just lay it on the line, lay it on the line, on that straight an' narrow line!'

"'Hallelujah, hallelujah, that's the Gospel truth!'

"Well, gentlemen, Ah don't reckon as Ah know how many folks was saved right then and there. Ah know we had more folks a comin' forward at the altar call to get saved then than all the other sermons combined. Lordy, what a time, what a time!

"Why, so many o' them poor souls came to Jesus that when we had a baptizin' towards the end of the meetin' down in the Greystone, don't you know, we plumb muddied up that water for nigh on an hour after'ards. The crystal-clear waters of the Greystone, all muddy as if stained by the washed off transgressions of all those sinners. I don't reckon as there's ever been a meetin' as powerful, afore or after, least ways not in Derry County."

We shook our heads in amazement and laughed.

"That's quite a story, Brother Hopkins. Quite a story," said Pastor Snider.

Jessica peeked into the room, and seeing we were just talking and not praying, she and a young man brought in our food and refilled our drinks.

"Anything else, Gentlemen?" asked Jessica.

Brother Hopkins senior said, "No, I think we're good, honey. Be sure and tell your maw and grandmaw I was here and said hello."

"Sure thing, Brother Hopkins." She left with a big smile.

We ate for a while in companiable silence. Then Reverend Nelson said, "You know, I seemed to have heard about John Elden before." He thought for a moment. "Yes, I'm sure of it now. He was quite a legend in the Southeast District of the Missouri Conference."

"Yes, the bolt of cloth they cut him from has played out, for sure," said the old preacher, pushing his half-finished plate away. "But, thinkin' of Brother Elden, it reminds me of another brush arbor story, this 'un with the man that replaced him on his circuit, named Jelley—Noel Jelley."

"Now, this Reverend Jelley was about near as tall as Brother Elden, but he was as small around as Brother Elden was large. Had a surprisingly deep bass voice, though. Rail thin man, but he'd get excited with the best of us. When he'd get a wavin' and a stompin', he looked for all the world like some invisible force'as waving a broom stick at a bee. Lord, it was right comical to see. But, friends, that Brother Jelley, he could preach.

"There was a small Methodist church, outside of the old Cumberland Crossroads community. It's near New Dublin—you know where that is?"

"Yes," I said, "It's in Adair County. New Dublin's where the Irish folks moved to when the bushwhackers burned down the original Dublin during the Civil War. Old Dublin they call it now. Nothing left but burned-out shells and foundation stones."

"That's right. Not much left of Cumberland Crossroads, either. So, there was this country church, couldn't been more than a dozen or so families there. Faith Methodist it was called. It's been closed for a few years now, Reverend Nelson."

He nodded and asked the older man to go on.

"This church was where Brother Jelley was baptized and raised and where he was first licensed as a lay preacher. Later, when he was commissioned as a local pastor, he had the service right there. The district superintendent came, as well as a number of other Methodist ministers. More'n a few Baptist preachers as well.

"This service was so big, the little church couldn't handle all the folks. So, they decided to build a brush arbor there on the property next to the church. This was a smaller affair than what Ah was talkin' about afore, and fancier too. They took some logs and split 'em to make benches. They also took some sawdust and scattered it around to make a sorta floor and also an aisle for folks to come down at the altar call. That's why we used to say, when folks come forward for salvation, they'd 'walk the sawdust trail.'

"Anyways, the ordination service was a good'un. The superintendent didn't preach much more'n 20 minutes, but the other brothers pitched in to make up the deficit. After'ards, they laid hands on him an' prayed over him an' gave him a brand-new Bible. Big ol' affair, it was. Leather with brass bindings. Had to cost a fortune. After the preaching, they decided to take up a collection to help Brother Jelley buy a new suit of clothes and get the brakes on his car fixed so he could drive his circuit safely.

"While they'as a doin' that, a big woman, I mean big (don't recollect her name), stood up at the front and sang a 'special,'[7] *O, Come Angel Band.*" Brother Hopkins began to sing. His baritone voice was pleasant and only a little shaky. Not sure any of us at the table could have done any better.

"O, Come Ange-el Band,
Come and arou-ound me stand,
O, carry me away on your snow-white wings
To my immortal ho-ome.
O, carry me away on your snow-white wings
To my immortal home.

"Now, when she hit that first 'home,' she decided she was goin' to go up on a high note, up into the rafters, but there was, at this point, quite a startlement.

"Ah'm sure that rat snake in the brush ceiling had no intention of creatin' a spectacle. He was prob'bly just sleepin' in the shade of some tree—it bein' hot and all— and when they cut the trees and brush for the arbor, he was already there and just rode along. Ah don't know, maybe he jist wanted to get religion." He winked at this.

---

[7] In the Ozarks, pronounced "spatial."

"Now, some folks'll tell you snakes cain't hear, them havin' no ears an' all (Dr. Spring prob'bly tell me right), but that ol' snake musta heard somethin' 'cause he kinda draped hisself out of that brush ceiling and commenced lookin' around, tryin' to find out what all the commotion was about.

"'Lord!' he prob'bly said to hisself. 'What is all this noise?' He looked around the room takin' it all in an' decided to go a little lower down for a better view.

"Well, several things happened, one after t'other. First, that woman singer, when she saw the snake hangin' about lookin' over the venue, she forgot all about singin' high on 'ho-ome' and instead decided to make up her own words. Don't recall them bein' either sacred or musical.

"Second, the snake decided he had 'bout enough of all this and dropped down outta the ceiling to make good his escape. Well, he was hangin' right over Brother Jelley's head, who couldn't see him an' who wondered what all the commotion was about. When that snake dropped down, 'Plop!' he saw with sudden clarity the cause of the singer's impiety. Also, the snake landed on his new, special Bible.

"Third, well, I guess figurin' the snake needed that Bible more'n he did, he tossed the two more or less as a combined unit off the stage and accidentally right into the face of that poor woman. As you could guess, that big ol' Bible knocked the sister clean out, an' down she went to the floor carryin' the snake with her as an unwillin' passenger. After landin', the snake looked about, saw that folks seemed to be occupied with their own troubles an', not guessin' he was the cause thereof, he decided to get while the gettin' was good an' slipped under some benches and headed for the hills. Problem, though: there'as folks sittin' along them benches and they expressed considerable vocal astonishments at this turn of events. Makin' good his escape, the snake slithered off to parts unknown.

"Meanwhile, feeling sorry for his recent abandonment of the Holy Scriptures, Brother Jelley went to retrieve his

Bible. About this time, that woman singer comes to. She sees the brother standin' over her, a reachin' down, and misconstrues the whole state of affairs. Liftin' up the Bible from her reclinin' position, she whomped him across the top of his head, sendin' him flyin' back'ards towards the pulpit they set up. He struck the pulpit, which toppled over onto the superintendent, comin' fair to break his arm. Had it in a sling for days after. Him bein' a true godly man, he was able to contain his thunder when it came to words but when it came to action, well, he was what they'd call a follower of 'muscular Christianity,' an' shoved that pulpit off hisself and back over on Brother Jelley. He more-or-less successfully deflected it (though it broke his wrist—had his arm in a sling as well after that), but it struck against an empty bench. The bench, decidin' it was in an untenable position, fell back'ards, knockin' o'er its kin to the rear with it and in turn they struck out at the shins of their neighbors' passengers. Those folks commenced to whoopin' and hoppin' about like they was at some Pentecostal meetin'. Well, such a noise you never did hear.

"Well, they'd finally straightened out the mess, an' settin' things in order, an' Brother Jelley goin' about apologizing to one an' all, an' when he came to the woman . . .

"Oh, my Lord, I remember who she was now! Why she was Adelaide Cummins and she married poor ol' Brother Jelley that very year. How could I forget? Well, as Ah told you, my memory's not so good.

"So, anyhow, them two figured after what they'd been through that night, marriage'd be a piece of cake. Right happy they were too, though his thinness and her stoutness led to many a jest. They had five young'uns.

"Anyways, the superintendent figured ol' Jelley couldn't hardly mess anything up any more than this, so he appointed him to take Brother Elden's circuit."

We were all laughing well before the story was finished. Pastor Snider snorted sweet tea out of his nose and splashed the table in front of him. We laughed all the harder.

"O, Lord," laughed Pastor Snider, wiping his nose and mouth. "I don't think I've laughed so hard since the story about the funeral procession, Brother Hopkins."

The memory of that story got us all laughing even louder. Jessica stuck her head in to make sure all was okay, saw us laughing, and smiled at us before retreating.

"Well, Dad," said Brother Hopkins the younger, starting to get up. "I guess we've got to be going. Don't want to get you in trouble with maw."

We all expressed our disappointment and begged for at least one more story. The older man looked to his son. We could tell he'd dearly love to give us another tale.

"All right, Dad. But just one more." He sat back down. His father looked at him in gratitude, as did we all.

"Well, friends, so far I've been tellin' tales on my Methodist brothers, and it don't seem right that I shouldn't give a mention about us Baptists," he began.

"Now, this happened afore my time, mind you, back in the years followin' the Civil War, maybe 1870 or nearer 1875. Ah was told this by Brother Alfred Bueller, who was originally from one of those German Baptist communities up towards Salem, but he came here to take the charge here at First Baptist. Mighty preacher he was, maybe the best ever in these parts. He was a real young man back then an' must've been in his 70s or 80s when I knew him. Didn't have hardly a lick of a German accent till he got excited an' let me tell you brothers, when he'd get all worked up over the Devil and Hell, that accent'd flat come out! Ain't nothin' more scary'n being yelled at about Ol' Slewfoot and the lake o' fire by an old-fashioned German Baptist preacher. Lord!

"So, anyhow, they'as rebuildin' the county back then, fixin' what the bushwhackers an' jayhawkers burned down.

They purely left a mess for a truth. Brother Bueller built a new church. The old one was made of wood an' burned down in 1863. He built a new, strong church made of stone an' it lasted for many a year until it was blowed down, mostly, by the tornado in '54.

"Now, there was still some bushwhackers about in them days. The war bein' over, they couldn't pretend to fight for the Confed'racy. They jist fought for themselves, mostly burnin' an' murderin' an' takin' what they wanted from poor folks.

"One of them, a big, big man, was named Fess Calder. Fess was as mean as a timber rattler in molt. An' like a rattler in molt, he'd strike first an' take to reckonin' later. Fess decided raidin' little farms warn't big enough doin's for him. Instead, he got a gang 'round hisself of some purty worthless ne'er-do-wells, mostly former bushwhackers such as hisself, an' they commenced to robbin' banks.

"First 'un was over in Wilmot, at the Adair County State Bank. Got away with maybe $2,000, a heap of money in them days. Shot the guard, nigh on to killin' him. Then they went down to Johnson Corners an' hit the branch of the Derry County State Bank there. Didn't get more'n a few hundred dollars. Well, that made ol' Fess mad, an' he shot the guard, the teller, an' the manager. Shot 'em doornail dead.

"Fess then hit the main branch of Derry County State Bank in Providence. They had the payroll in for the lumber company, maybe $10-15,000 in all. He locked the tellers, the guard, and the manager in the manager's office an' set the place afire out of shear 'orneriness. The manager and all was able to escape, by the way. So, as Fess an' his gang was comin' out, well friends, Ah tell you, they was several kinds of loco. They commenced to shootin' up an' down the street. Wounded Doc Pritchett an' Virgil MacKay's daddy. But worst of all, they killed the little Vandervort baby in his pram. 'Course they didn't mean to kill that baby, not even Fess was that bad, but still . . .

"The Sheriff of Derry County (at the time I think he was a MacKay, Dr. Spring; don't recall his Christian name) formed a posse to track down ol' Fess an' his gang. Well, brothers, they fair rode 'round all over the county an' into Adair and Bean counties as well. They finally boxed him in one of them dead-end hollers down by Goliath Springs. They surrounded him with some good ol' boys, right fine riflemen they were, an' just proceeded to wait 'em out. The posse's sentinels probably shot an' killed two or three of 'em. The rest, they nearly starved out.

"Fess an' a couple of others decided to make a break for it an' show a brave face by runnin' out o' the holler right through the posse. Well, Sheriff MacKay was no fool, an' he had his men hunkered down behind logs an' rocks an' such. They just blazed away at Fess an' his boys. Killed all but Fess hisself. Turned out he was powerfully shot up, but none of them wounds was deadly serious. Ol' Doc Pritchett, gun-shot though he was, patched him up proper an', by-an'-by, he got well enough to stand trial.

"They thought they had him locked up purty tightly in the old Derry County jail, which sat next to the ol' court-house. But it was made of logs an' somehow or t'other, he managed to escape. He was caught afore he even left Providence. Guess folks'as on the lookout. He tried to escape a couple more times but didn't get nary as far as the first attempt.

"Well, the state attorney said, this is it, no more escapin'. Fess was shackled to a long ol' iron stake driven through the floorboards of the jail an' into the ground below. He was to be under guard 24 hours an' never allowed to leave the cell. Had to do his bus'ness in front of the guard, an' I reckon a 12-gauge shotgun an' a tin bucket made that right hard.

"They tried him as soon as the district judge an' the state attorney could come down. Well, that took a while 'cause, bein' such a notorious case, every judge and prosecutor in the state wanted a shot at it. Finally, the governor hisself stepped in an' sent a judge from St. Louis and the deputy state attorney general. Took more'n two months to get that sorted.

"They tried Fess in the Derry County Courthouse. It was July and it was plum hot an' they had the windows open, but, by-an'-by, there was so many folks a standin' 'round outside of the courthouse, a yammerin' an' a goin' on, that the judge ordered the windows closed. After the first day with the judge, the jury an' the attorneys gettin' parboiled, the judge orders the trial to be held early in the morning an' late in the evenin'. It was cooler then, 'course, but also most folks had chores then, so it grew powerfully quieter an' they could open the windows.

"So, they went through the witnesses, them all a tellin' what a wicked an' lawless man Fess was. When poor ol' Mrs. Vandervort took the stand, why there was not a dry eye in the court, 'ceptin' Fess. When Fess was called to give an account for hisself, he jist spat at the state attorney an' said not a word. 'Course, the jury found him guilty of murder, attempted murder, and robbin' state-chartered banks, and there was no other sentence that could be passed 'cept death by hangin'.

"Well, after the trial, the only person other than the guards, the sheriff, or the state attorney they'd allow to see him was Brother Bueller. At first, Fess didn't have no truck with him. But by-an'-by, his words about the awful judgment awaitin' him on t'other side, an' how that the Savior could rescue even such a one as him, got Fess to thinkin' right hard about religion.

"One day, Brother Bueller was fair shoutin' at Fess about the horrors of Hell an' that German accent came out. 'You vant to die und go to Hell? Come, schtupider zinner! Ist das vat you vant! You vant der Teufel to schtab you mit his pitchfork in your arsche? Und eat your nüssen mit his great sharp teeths?'

"Well, Fess Calder threw hisself on the floor an' began a cryin' out, 'Lord, save me! Help me, Jesus! Ah'm a wretched sinner! Ah don't deserve the mercy o' man or God! Please, Jesus, please! Forgive this poor ol' transgressor!'

"So, Brother Bueller commenced to tellin' him the Gospel, in a right gentle tone, an' how he could get right with God, even though he'd be a hangin' from the gallows soon. The judgment of man he could not escape, said he, but the judgment of God he could avoid through Jesus an' Him crucified. So, he led that sinner in prayer for the forgiveness of sins an' salvation by the blood.

"Brothers, this seemed to be the real deal. 'Course, cain't tell the true state of a man's soul, but Brother Bueller allowed as to how he thought Fess Calder was truly converted. Oh, most folks thought it was all a show or just him hedgin' his bets, so to speak.

"Well, that o' course meant there'as one more thing to do: Fess was needin' to be baptized—an' baptized right (beggin' you gentlemen's pardon), dunked clean under in water in the name of the Father, the Son, and the Holy Ghost.

"In those days, most all baptizin' was in a creek or river or a pond. So, Brother Bueller asked the sheriff if he could take Fess Calder, under escort, o' course, down to the Greystone to wash ol' Fess' sins away.

"Well, the sheriff wasn't too keen on the idea, but he allowed as how he'd ask the county judge. The judge likewise wasn't too enthusiastic, but said he'd telegraph the state attorney's office.

"As you can imagine, the state attorney shut down that idea as quick as a duck on a June bug. 'There's no way in tarnation that that murderous 'so-and-so' (I'm sure his words were a might more crude than that) is to be let off that chain an' shackle an' out of that jail until the day of his execution.'

"So, Brother Bueller protested that as a new convert to the faith, Fess Calder had to be baptized by full immersion. The state attorney said he didn't care. Let Fess become a

Methodist an' they could sprinkle him in the cell. Well, Fess determined as how he had but this last river to cross an' he was not about to change horses in mid-stream, going from Baptist to Methodist, an' Brother Bueller strongly agreed.

"'Vat do zey mean, becoming a Methodist? I vent to zeh problem of converting zat murderer and und now zhe Methodist gets him und der credit? Donner vetter! Gott in Himmel!'

"Well, with the full weight of Brother Bueller's German anger pouring out on him, the sheriff felt obliged to help him out somehow. So, he came up with a scheme: they have the town barrel maker, a Mr. Robards, as I recall, make up a big wash tub—big enough to dunk ol' Fess, iff'n he sat down to begin with.

"Brother Bueller agreed as how that would pay the bill. So, the sheriff went to Mr. Robards an' asked iff'n he was willin' to build the contraption. Well, as you kin imagine, he was a fair piece leery of the project, but the sheriff promised him twice his normal price for the tub, and that Fess would be shackled and under the shotgun-totin' observation o' two deputies, so he agreed.

"When he got to the jail and saw how big Fess was up that close, an' how narrow the cell door was, he was a might consternated. He allowed as how he would have to build that tub in the cell—there was no way he could build it at his cooper's shop an' tote it into the cell. It'd be too big and heavy for one and they'd never be able to get it through the door for another. He also expressed his considerable reluctance to be in such close proximity to such a hardened criminal, regardless of the condition of his soul. He didn't want ol' Fess to go backsliding on his head when he wasn't lookin'.

"The sheriff understood, o' course. Fess gave him the fantods as well, even bein' armed with a shotgun an' a Colt revolver. So, the sheriff said he'd bring the blacksmith over to temporarily shorten Fess' chain and move the iron stake into the corner.

"Well, as you kin imagine, ol' Fess wasn't too keen on the idea, but Brother Bueller told him, in so many words, beggars cain't be choosers. So, off Fess went into the corner, chained up short, guarded closely by them two deputies.

"So, Mr. Robards commenced to work. He got some oak barrel staves, figurin' this tub'd need to be stout. He determined as how since Fess was all of six foot two or more, he'd need to make that tub at least six feet to get Fess dunked completely startin' from a sittin' position. He made careful measurements, had the blacksmith pound out a couple of custom hoops and bradded the whole thing together, puttin' oakum between the staves.

"Come the day, there was Brother Bueller an' the two deputies in the cell (an' Fess, of course), an' the sheriff, the county judge, an' a reporter from the *Greystone Local* standin' just outside. An' in the center o' that cell, purty nigh takin' up all the floor which wasn't stood upon, was that tub.

"Earlier in the day, the deputies filled the tub with water from the Greystone. Purty near as cold as ice, Ah'm sure it seemed to Fess. Brother Bueller asked if they couldn't warm it somewhat on the stove, but the Sheriff said, nah, seein's how Fess escaped the fires o' hell, it was only appropriate he get dunked in the opposite condition. Brother Bueller prob'bly agreed. Least ways he didn't make a fuss about it none. He had ol' Fess strip down to his long johns and sit-down careful like in the center of the tub. Fess started to complain about how cold the water was, but nobody paid him no never-mind.

"Brother Bueller began to question Fess. 'Do you acknowledge yer a coal-black stained sinner in need o' God's grace an' forgiveness?' Fess allowed as he did, though it was hard to hear him, what with his teeth a chatterin' so.

"'Do you repent of yer sins and ask fer God's forgiveness?' Again, Fess gave his feeble response in the affirmative.

"'And do you put yer full faith an' trust in Jesus Christ an' him alone for yer salvation?' Fess said somethin' along the lines of yes, an' could they please get along with it.

"'Very well,' proclaims the preacher, 'Fess Calder, Ah baptize you in the name of the Father, an' in the name of the . . .'

"Well, along about here there was an important discovery made an' the discovery had its roots in an oversight by Mr. Robards. When you make a barrel, you gotta pour water into it to swell up them staves an' the oakum an' get a good tight fit. Might have to do that a couple o' times. Well, Robards forgot to do that. Small wonder, him bein' all nervous about bein' in the proximity of such a cold-blooded killer.

"So, when Brother Bueller commenced to leaning Fess back, why, friends he never got to 'Son,' never mind 'an' in the name of the Holy Ghost,' 'cause it was about then that the staves gave way and that water sloshed all over. It got everyone, even those outside the cell, a good bit wet. The deputies and Brother Bueller was completely dowsed, from head to toe. An' there was poor ol' Fess, sittin' on the floor of that tub, chatterin' his teeth and a hollerin', sayin' as how he was left in his sins an' was a goin' to hell 'cause of it.

"Well, Brother Bueller saw Fess was plum wet through, and that all over, from the crown of his head to the soles of his feet, so, he reckoned as how this counted for a full immersion. He continued, '. . . an' in the name of the Son, an' in the name o' the Holy Ghost. Amen.'

"Ordinarily, the congregation s'pposed to say 'Amen' in response, but they was too wet and startled to say aught. So, Brother Bueller said a mighty short prayer and told Fess his baptism was complete. Fess grinned in relief, though his face was blue with the cold. One of the deputies had an ol' stiff, raggedy towel he brought in for Fess. He handed it to Fess without much thinkin' an' then realized everyone else was goin' to be left in their water-logged condition. The sheriff told the deputies to keep a guardin' Fess while he an' everyone else could squelch back home to dry off an' change their clothes. He said he'd come back later to relieve them one at a time so they could go home and do the same.

"Later, on his way back, he stopped at the cooper's an' let him know in no uncertain terms he could go to the jail an' pick up the pieces of his worthless barrel. He cussed Robards an' his tub a blue streak, Ah'm sure. Said he wasn't goin' to pay for it, neither, what with it bein' a worthless piece of work, an' that he should be right glad he didn't arrest him for conspir'cy to assault four officers of the court an' a man o' the cloth. Didn't say aught 'bout the reporter. Well, Robards face dropped to about the floor an', friends, if he didn't go about hang-dawg for the rest o' the month.

"Next day, they led ol' Fess to the gallows. The whole county an' nigh on to half of Adair County was there to see him off. Brother Bueller got up an' preached a sermon on hellfire an' damnation but as to how God would forgive even the blackest o' sinners iff'n he'd only repent, which he assured the crowd ol' Fess had.

"The judge asked if Fess had any last words. Fess stood there lookin' both peaceful an' powerfully sorrowful. He told folks how he was such a terrible transgressor o' the laws of God and man, an' he was a gettin' nothin' but what he deserved. He thanked God for His forgiveness an' thanked Brother Bueller for showin' him the right way.

"Then they put the noose around Fess' neck. Ah don't need to tell you boys what happened after that, exceptin' the hangin' was all regular like accordin' to plan.

"So ended the life of ol' Fess Calder—a murderer, an' a thief, but who made his peace with his God."

We all murmured that this was a fine story, a good note to end on, reminding us of just how powerful the grace of God is.

The younger Brother Hopkins stood and said, "Well, Dad, I reckon that's enough for the day. Thank you, gentlemen, for your kind attention."

Brother Hopkins senior said he was grateful to us for listening to his stories. We all said that we were thankful for his time.

I left the Riverside and headed to my parked car so I could drive over to Wilmot to get Elsbeth. I called Elsbeth on my mobile phone and asked her if she was finished shopping. She said she was, that she found a knick-knack or two, but nothing more. She told me she would wait in the little tea shop next to the antiques store.

Two weeks later, I got a call from Brother John Hopkins.

"Dr. Spring?"

"Yes, is this Brother Hopkins? I recognize your voice."

"Yes, it is. Listen, I just wanted to tell you Dad died in Columbia yesterday. Passed away quietly in his sleep."

I remarked that, since I knew he was in the presence of Jesus, I wasn't sorry for his dad, but I knew the family was grieving and I offered my condolences.

"Thank you," he said. "Listen, I want you to know how much it meant to him for Pastor Snider, Reverend Nelson, and you to listen so attentively to his stories. He was so happy. Went around singing old revival hymns to himself all the rest of the day."

"Oh, Brother Hopkins, I can assure you that I was blessed—so very much—by that time. I'm sure he received an angel-chorus welcome and a star-filled crown when he went to meet Jesus."

"Yes, and knowing Dad, he was powerfully joyful to cast that crown at the Savior's feet. Good-bye, Dr. Spring. May the good Lord bless you and yours."

"Thank you, Brother Hopkins. And may Christ bless you and your family as well. Say hi to the folks in Providence for me. Good-bye."

Nine: The Road out of Derry County

Green Tea and Honey

The shadows were lengthening across the room when he turned off the computer. He didn't like to write in the evenings. He grew too sentimental and maudlin, his writing as well. Too many memories. He looked up to watch the fading sunlight taking its last peek through the window. Without thinking, he got up, closed the curtains, crossed the room to the switch, started to turn on the overhead light, but decided not to.

Instead, he turned on the lamp on the small table by his old, nearly worn-out recliner. The chair was old because he was too cheap to by a new one. It was perfectly good after all. Nearly worn-out because it was comfortable, like an old friend. It wasn't that he couldn't afford a new recliner. Elsbeth's insurance money, their investments, Social Security, and his military retirement pay left him well off. It's just that, well, he was cheap. "Probably too much Scottish blood," he mused, surveying the worn and discolored arms and seat. He threw a patchwork quilt over it when company came, which wasn't often. Mostly just when the grandkids visited.

Living by himself in the Missouri Ozarks suited him just fine. A snug little stone and timber house next to the National Forest, where he could hike to his heart's content.

Close enough to the little town of Johnson Corners to spend time with folks, when he wanted to, at the faux 1930s diner. Far enough away when he didn't want to. It was a bit far from the kids, but they saw him at Thanksgiving or Christmas and for a couple of weeks during the summer.

He stretched his long frame, straightened his rumpled plaid flannel shirt and forest green cardigan, and rambled around the book-lined living room, into the well-appointed kitchen (her doing), trying to remember something he hadn't really forgotten. More habit than anything else. He opened a cabinet, got down a tumbler, and poured himself a glass of water. "That well water sure tastes good," he thought after downing it. He poured himself another glass and drank it, making sure to leave just the tiniest amount at the bottom, just enough left for the bourbon.

Returning to the living room, he got out the bottle of bourbon ("Expensive stuff, something I'm not cheap about"), poured himself a double, and sat down in the chair. Taking care to set the glass down on a coaster on the small table next to him, he reached into his cardigan pocket, got out his pipe and tobacco, and meditatively fiddled with them. Satisfied it was packed right, he lit a match from the box he kept on the table, and he puffed carefully, thoughtfully, getting the right draw.

Being able to smoke inside the house was about the only thing that was "good" about her being gone, his wife of more than 50 years. He sighed at the memory of them sitting companionably in the evenings, watching old movies on the TV. They also liked watching travelogues about places exotic and far away. They had talked about maybe going someday, Peru, India, maybe back to England. He always wanted to take the Rhine-Danube River Cruise. They never got around to it. And now they never would.

Every so often, he'd get out the multi-colored travel brochures they got at the travel agency in Oakmont. He thought he might go ahead and travel alone, now that she was gone.

Maybe go to those places they talked about. Maybe take a couple of his oldest grandkids with him (what were they now, in their late twenties?). Maybe. But inertia had hold of him and wasn't likely to let go anytime soon.

He sat and watched the smoke curling up to the ceiling. "Gonna have to paint that someday, getting yellow." Taking a sip of his bourbon, he nearly dropped the glass, startled by a knock at the door.

"Who in the world could that be?"

He strode to the door, turned on the porch light, and opened the door cautiously. "Can't be too careful when it's getting dark."

Standing outside was a small, blonde, teenage girl, maybe 16 or 17. Eighteen at the oldest. She was dressed in a flannel shirt, jeans, and sandals and was holding a wide-brimmed straw hat. She was soaking wet, and water was pouring down from her onto the porch. "Odd, it isn't raining."

"Hi, mister," she said through chattering teeth. "I've had an accident down by the river and fell in. I'm so cold. Can I come in to get dry?" Despite her state, she said this in a way which was both apologetic and oddly confident as though, of course, he'd let her in.

Wordlessly, he held the door open for her and indicated the bathroom. "Use the shower, if you like, to warm up. You'll find towels in the cabinet and a robe on the back of the door. It's mine, so it'll be big on you, but I washed it just this morning. I'll make you some hot tea."

She thanked him quietly and dripped across the floor. "I'm sorry about the mess," she said softly, and slipped into the bathroom. In a moment, he heard the shower turn on.

He moved into the kitchen, filled the kettle, set it on a burner, and turned on the gas stove. He set out a big mug, put in a bag of green tea ("Probably like that, most young girls do"), and got the honey out of the pantry. He was out of cream, he hoped that was okay.

Just as the kettle began to whistle, the girl stepped almost silently into the room. She was swamped in his robe, hair damp and stringy, almost impossible to make anything out but her face, but there was something about the way she moved . . .

"I left my clothes in the bathtub, I hope that's okay." There was that odd note in her voice of both apology and confidence again, as though she knew the answer would be, "Of course that's okay." She drew out a kitchen chair and sat down at the table. He set the steeping tea and the honey in front of her.

"I'm sorry, I'm out of cream."

"It's alright, I like this fine. And honey goes so well in green tea, at least I think so. Do you?"

"Well, my wife thought so. I'm more of a coffee person." He drew out a chair and sat opposite her. He looked into her eyes, the color of the pool at Blue Springs. Somehow, she looked familiar.

"Your wife, is she here?"

A strange, odd tingle went down his chest and settled momentarily in his stomach and was gone.

"No, she died a few years back."

"May I ask how, or is that too painful?"

Ordinarily, he avoided the story of Elsbeth's death, but for some reason it seemed right, even necessary, to tell it, to get it out there in the open. Slowly, hesitantly, he shared with her.

"We were canoeing down the Cave River. I took the sharp-bend left-hand fork down below Dancehall Cave. Couldn't see ahead. There was a huge sycamore tree blown down across the stream. The current was going way too fast. We slammed into the tree. The canoe overturned and swamped. She fell out and was washed down stream, calling to me."

He halted a moment to collect himself. "I guess I bashed my head into the tree, dazed me. I dove under the tree and swam after her. I was too late. Found her in a willow strainer. Even with her life jacket on she got caught up in the roots. Drowned."

He stared off into space as if he was reliving the events over and over in his mind. "I've never forgiven myself." He took in a slow deep breath and let it out even slower. A tear trickled down his cheek.

She reached over and touched his hand. That same, tiny electric thrill came back.

"That's so sad," she said, sounding as if she was sharing his grief. She paused, seeming to carefully measure her next words. "But you have to forgive yourself. It was an accident. They can happen so easily, especially down on the Cave. That's where I fell in."

He looked up, his eyes blurry. Her deep blue eyes met his. He gasped suddenly with recognition. He knew those eyes. So long ago, back when Elsbeth and he first fell in love.

He shook his head in confusion and disbelief. The single tear became a flood. "What? How? O God!"

"Alastair, honey, it's okay. It's okay." She leaned over, touched his face, wiping away the tears. "I forgive you. Well, there's nothing to forgive, really. Let go. Move on." And then, after the shortest of pauses, "I love you, Alastair."

He put his head in his hands and cried loud, quivering sobs. Again, he felt her hand caress his cheek. She kissed him on the back of his neck. Then silence. He looked up. She was gone.

He scanned the room in confusion. The robe lay neatly folded on the chair, as though he just folded it fresh out of the dryer. The mug sat on the table, untouched. His was the only chair pulled out from the table. He got up and staggered around the cottage looking for her. No sign of her, no wet footprints on the floor, no wet clothes lying in the tub, it wasn't even damp. He ran to the door, threw it open, and looked out into the moonlit Ozark night. Nothing. She couldn't have gone that far.

He ran back inside, hurriedly got a flashlight, put on some walking shoes, and headed into the moon-silvered dark. Calling, calling her name—

"Elsbeth! Elsbeth!"

No answer. No shadowy shape in the distance. No sound except the slightest of whispers in the pines. He stumbled down the gravel road in front of his house all the way down to the river. There was no sign of her.

He slowly returned home. "She was so beautiful, like she was many years ago, like it was just yesterday."

Arriving at the cottage, he shut the door (but left the porch light on, just in case), and threw himself into his chair, dropping the still-lit flashlight to the floor, not bothering to take off his dusty shoes. He sat trembling for a long time.

Sometime later, maybe minutes, maybe hours, maybe decades, he didn't know, he reflexively reached over, took up the flashlight, and turned it off. He picked up the bourbon and drained the tumbler. He got up and turned off the table light. "Might as well go to bed." Finishing his nighttime routine, without turning on the bedroom light, he crept to the bed, and slipped between the cool, freshly laundered sheets. He felt an odd lightness in his head, as though something happened he had long waited for.

"In the morning," he said sleepily, "I'm going to call the travel agent."

One Last Hike

"Dad, are you okay?"

He started slightly, coming to from his reverie.

"What?" he asked.

"I asked if you're okay."

He looked at his daughter, Naomi, noting the concern tracing her pretty face.

"Why do you ask?"

"Well, you've been holding that book for at least five minutes."

He looked down at the book in his hands. It was a well-worn paperback, a comic drawing on the much-creased cover. A book well read, well loved. The Penguin edition of P.G. Wodehouse's *Lord Emsworth and Others*. He recalled hours of laughter, hours of the warm glow of listening to Elsbeth, his late wife, read it, well, as best she could between her own bouts of laughter.

"Oh, I'm okay, Naomi, just a lot of memories."

She smiled quietly and took the book from him, her own reminiscences lighting her face.

"We did have a lot of fun with this old book. Look at how beat-up it is."

He laughed softly. "Yes, and that's like the third copy we bought. Just kept wearing it out. I bet there's more than a few smudges on those pages from your mom laughing so hard she started crying."

His daughter gave the book one last look and placed it in a box marked "Books—Keep."

He remembered now what they were doing, and he sighed. Going through his library, setting aside his textbooks and other scientific volumes to send to the university, keeping the well-thumbed field guides, and winnowing his novels and short-story collections down to the few he was likely to read again. He hated giving away books. Well, no, that's not true. He gave away a lot of books to friends, works that he treasured: *King Solomon's Ring, Mere Christianity, Ortho-*

doxy, The Lord of the Rings, The Hobbit, At Home in Mitford, and such. But with those, he always made sure he had an extra copy on the shelf.

He surveyed the shelves in the formerly book-lined living room. Mostly empty now. About half of the volumes were in boxes marked "University," the rest in the "keep" boxes or in small stacks on the floor, stacks which he promised he'd go through soon to make a final decision.

"I'm tired, baby girl. Can we finish this later?"

She knew that this was going to be the hardest part of moving. She had come over from near Springfield with her kids (Kids? Both in their thirties now with kids of their own) to help him pack up the little stone and timber house in the Ozarks and move him to live with her.

"You'll love it, Dad. We live right next to the State Forest. There's wildlife and trails and so many birds. And we've got a little apartment all your own downstairs with an exterior door."

Truth was, she'd been concerned about him for quite some time. It'd been 20 years since her mom died, and he was in his early nineties now. He was healthy (well, for a man his age), but a bit unsteady in his balance and often prone to long, distracted silences. The doctor didn't think he had dementia, just a long life with so many experiences to relive in his mind and heart. Still, she worried about him, and wondered how long it would be before he lost his way in his beloved forest, despite it being well-remembered by him. With no one there to watch over him, he might be gone for days, might never return home.

"And Dad, I'm not sending the Forest Service people after you! You get lost, you get back on your own!"

He knew she didn't mean it, but he also saw the sense in leaving—leaving his beloved hills, his well-fished streams, his much-treasured trails; trails where it seemed he knew every tree, every rock, every hollow. But also leaving behind his daughter's concerns and fears.

His biggest sorrow was leaving Elsbeth behind. She wasn't really there, in that simple grave in the MacKay family cemetery on the hill looking over Derry Creek, but the powerful ghost of the memory of her would haunt him everywhere he went until the day when he would finally be laid to rest in that gravelly clay soil next to her.

"Sure, Dad, we can finish this tomorrow morning. Why don't you lie down and take a short nap?"

"No, don't feel like a nap." He stretched out the kink that developed in his back from stooping down to pack boxes. "I think I'll take a short hike. Maybe a mile or two. Might be my last, after all, what with the movers coming tomorrow afternoon."

"I don't know, how much day light is left? I don't want you losing your way in the dark."

"Honey, there's plenty of day left, maybe three or four hours. Besides, I'm just going to walk down to the river and back. And don't worry, I'll keep away from the bank," addressing the worry he knew was in her mind.

"Okay, but don't go too far. I'll be making dinner in a couple of hours, and I don't want it to get cold."

He smiled broadly by way of acknowledgment, grabbed his beat-up green oilskin fedora and sassafras walking stick, and headed jauntily out the door. After a hundred yards or so, though, he slowed down. "This will be my last time."

He looked at the well-worn trail and overarching trees with sad appreciation. He heard the cardinals singing and the wind whispering in the pines. He smelled the buttery aroma of the sycamores down by the river and the rich loamy smell of the forest floor layered with needles, and fallen cones, and branches. "Goodbye, old friends. Goodbye. You've kept me company all those long years. And when she died, you were there to sigh and mourn with me. Goodbye."

He walked about a half mile along the path, the river just to his right, singing her laughing song of splashes on the rocks, dancing trout, and ghostly herons wading in the eddies. He suddenly felt very tired.

"Maybe she was right, maybe I should've taken that nap. I think I'll sit down here for a minute."

He carefully lowered himself at the base of an enormous, aged post oak, a tree he knew like a next-door neighbor. "Pretty much is," he mused. Settling himself in a nook between two massive roots, he leaned back against the trunk and sighed with contentment.

"Mustn't sit here too long, or I'll be in trouble. Just a couple of minutes." But drowsiness caught him in its pleasant embrace, and before he knew it, he was fast asleep.

He awoke with a start. "Lord, I hope I wasn't asleep too long! I'll be in trouble for sure!"

"Of course, you won't be, silly man."

Startled, he looked up. The sun, which was well down in the west when he sat down, was in the east now, maybe two hours or so after dawn. The light pirouetted in and amongst the leaves as though choreographed in the most intricate, breath-catching allemande. There was a wonderful, swirling opera of birds calling, joined by a river chorus, and the wind singing a lilting aria in the branches overhead. And there she was.

"Come on, tall man. We've got a trail to hike." She smiled brightly, her dancing face and eyes free of the cares and toils of time, leaving her more beautiful than ever in her old life.

She held out a hand, a hand warm and soft and strong with youth and pulled him up as though he weighed less than a feather, and, in truth, he felt that light and dance-y, as though the slightest breeze would spring away with him.

"You sure we got time?" he asked.

"Honey, we got all the time we need and then some."

They walked hand and hand down the trail.

About the Author

In a time when most think of Renaissance men as old Italian dudes found in the pages of politically incorrect textbooks for Western Civ 2, Mark Allen Quay belies this view *con una vendetta.*

Quay was an intelligence analyst, medical response planner for nuclear war and cataclysmic natural disasters, high school science teacher, theology professor, exorcist, school headmaster, pastor, top secret courier, international consultant to government and church officials, theological seminary dean, world traveler, hospital administrator, missionary, and adventurer (the guy would hang off cliffs on ropes and belly-crawl through caves, for crying out loud).

He is a descendent of some of the first European settlers in the Ozarks, Anglican priest and canon (no, not cannon, loose or otherwise), natural historian, storyteller, retired Air Force officer, author of five books (including a minor bestseller about "things that go bump in the night") and numerous scholarly articles, hiker and backpacker, award-winning poet, and ridiculously over-educated with two doctorates. And the weirdest thing of all? It's all true.

Though both are from the Ozarks, after twelve previous moves, he and his long-suffering wife, Jani, currently make their home in Alabama. They have three adult children (Nordic-looking overachievers, the lot of them) and seven grandchildren, all of whom are very good looking and mostly very loud. He is owned by two cats—an enormous bobtail and a complaining tortoiseshell.

www.MarkAllenQuay.com